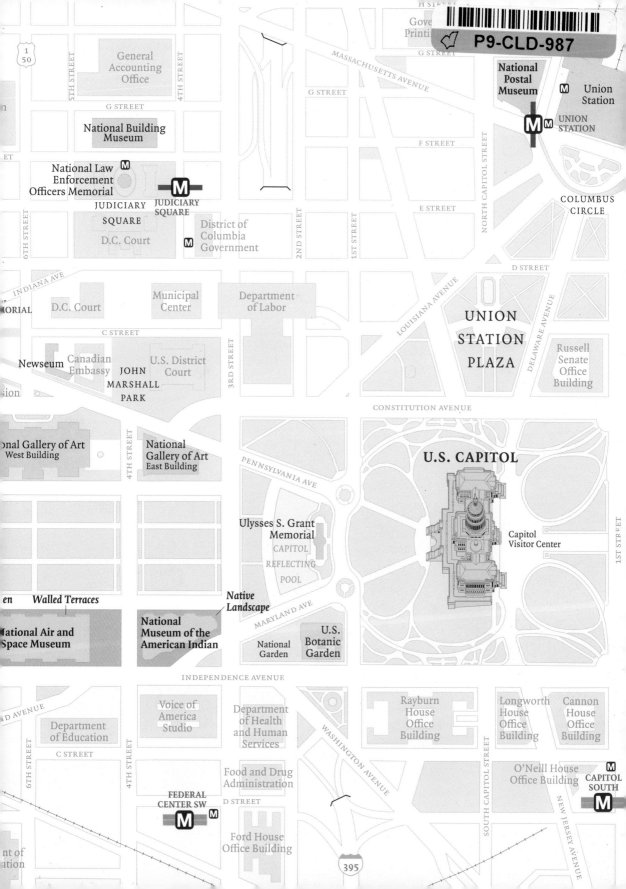

General Accounting Office

5TH STREET

4TH STREET

1 50

MASSACHUSETTS AVENUE

Gove Printi

G STREET

H STREET

G STREET

National Postal Museum

Union Station

UNION STATION

National Building Museum

National Law Enforcement Officers Memorial

JUDICIARY SQUARE

JUDICIARY SQUARE

F STREET

E STREET

NORTH CAPITOL STREET

COLUMBUS CIRCLE

6TH STREET

D.C. Court

District of Columbia Government

2ND STREET

1ST STREET

D STREET

INDIANA AVE

D.C. Court

Municipal Center

Department of Labor

3RD STREET

LOUISIANA AVENUE

UNION STATION PLAZA

DELAWARE AVENUE

Russell Senate Office Building

MORIAL

C STREET

Newseum

Canadian Embassy

JOHN MARSHALL PARK

U.S. District Court

CONSTITUTION AVENUE

sion

nal Gallery of Art West Building

4TH STREET

National Gallery of Art East Building

PENNSYLVANIA AVE

U.S. CAPITOL

Capitol Visitor Center

1ST STREET

Ulysses S. Grant Memorial

CAPITOL

REFLECTING

POOL

en   Walled Terraces

Native Landscape

MARYLAND AVE

National Air and Space Museum

National Museum of the American Indian

National Garden

U.S. Botanic Garden

INDEPENDENCE AVENUE

D AVENUE

Department of Education

C STREET

6TH STREET

Voice of America Studio

4TH STREET

Department of Health and Human Services

Food and Drug Administration

FEDERAL CENTER SW

D STREET

Ford House Office Building

WASHINGTON AVENUE

Rayburn House Office Building

Longworth House Office Building

Cannon House Office Building

SOUTH CAPITOL STREET

O'Neill House Office Building

CAPITOL SOUTH

NEW JERSEY AVENUE

nt of ation

395

A GUIDE TO SMITHSONIAN
GARDENS

CAROLE OTTESEN

Smithsonian Books · Washington

This publication has been prepared by Smithsonian Books in association with Smithsonian
Gardens, Barbara Faust, Associate Director.

Funding for this book was provided in part by
the Smithsonian Institution Scholarly Press.

Produced by Smithsonian Books
Carolyn Gleason, Director
Caroline Newman, Executive Editor
Christina Wiginton, Project Editor
Michelle Lecuyer, Editorial Assistant

Text by Carole Ottesen

Edited by Diane Maddex, Archetype Press

Designed by Robert L. Wiser

Library of Congress
Cataloging-in-Publication Data

Ottesen, Carole, 1942–
A guide to Smithsonian gardens /
Carole Ottesen.
   p.   cm.
ISBN 978-1-58834-300-0
1. Smithsonian Institution.
2. Gardens—Washington (D.C.) I. Title.
SB466.U65W37 2011
712.09753—dc22

        2010031276

First Edition

16   15   14   13   12   11   5   4   3   2   1

Printed in China
through Oceanic Graphic Printing, Inc.

Smithsonian Books titles may be purchased
for educational, business, or sales promotional
use. For information, please write:

Special Markets Department
Smithsonian Books
P.O. Box 37012, MRC 513
Washington, D.C. 20013-7012

Display photographs:
Page 1: A lamppost in the Enid A. Haupt
Garden (fashioned after a historic Georgetown
model) supports a basket of annuals and
cascading dark purple sweet potato vine
(Ipomea batatas 'Blackie'). A green star-
shaped yucca plant (Yucca rostata)
contrasts with the Castle's red sandstone.
Pages 2–3: The ornate doors at the Castle's
east entrance open onto the Kathrine Dulin
Folger Rose Garden. Page 4: A dragonfly
alights on the bud of a lotus (Nelumbo
nucifera) in a wetland at the National Zoo.
Page 5: Jewel-like drops of dew glisten on a
spider web attached to the needles of a mugo
pine (Pinus mugo var. pumilo) (top).
Fragrant and beautiful, Oriental lilies
(Lilium 'Black Beauty') are some of the many
delights found throughout the Smithsonian
gardens in the summer (bottom).

Because the nature of gardens is ephemeral,
plants growing in the Smithsonian gardens at
the time of publication will change.

Contents

FOREWORD

My daily walk to work takes me through the small but luxuriant Mary Livingston Ripley Garden, located between the grand old Arts and Industries Building and the modern Hirshhorn Museum and Sculpture Garden. Once I am inside my office on the second floor of the Smithsonian Castle, four twelve-foot-high Palladian windows provide me with generous views that I am thankful for each day. Looking eastward, our nation's Capitol majestically rises above the vibrant colors of the Kathrine Dulin Folger Rose Garden. To the south, the beauty of the Enid A. Haupt Garden fills my windows. All of this comes with its own whimsical music, as the Smithsonian carousel gently whirls laughing children round and round and sends forth patriotic tunes from its calliope.

My expansive office views allow me to appreciate the powerful effect the Smithsonian gardens have on our visitors. You can spot the serious gardeners: They know that the gardens are something special and carefully begin reading the labels. Then they take photographs, first from a distance, then steadily moving into close-ups, and eventually creeping into the gardens on hands and knees. These gardens affect even the most casual visitors, whose families use them as backdrops for photographs and whose children play in the water of the fountains. I like to think that photographs by garden experts and casual visitors alike remain part of a family's memory long after their visit to the Smithsonian.

Now these memories will be enhanced and preserved with Carole Ottesen's insightful book, *A Guide to Smithsonian Gardens*. "The Smithsonian experience does not begin and end at the doors of its museums," she correctly observes. "Beyond the museum walls are gardens and interior courtyards that have been designed to augment and complement the collections within."

Credit for our beautiful and diverse gardens goes to a remarkable group of horticultural experts who are passionate about their work. They know that the gardens must look special each day because our visitors may come here only once. They work through adversity when the elements threaten the gardens, and they are here long hours when needed. I am grateful to those who are here today and those who came before for creating the majesty of our gardens, and I am delighted that Carole Ottesen has preserved the fascinating story of our gardens in print.

Surprise and delight await those who take the time to look beyond our museums to our gardens, and this book is the perfect guide to enhance the journey. Enjoy!

G. Wayne Clough, Secretary
Smithsonian Institution

Purple petunias (Petunia × hybrida) ring a living version of the Smithsonian's sunburst symbol (opposite), executed in yellow Joseph's coat (Alternanthera ficoidea 'True Yellow'). William Wetmore Story's 1882 statue of the Smithsonian's first secretary, Joseph Henry, stands in front of the Castle.

Located between the Arts and Industries Building and the Hirshhorn Museum and Sculpture Garden, the Mary Livingston Ripley Garden (overleaf) displays hundreds of varieties of annual and perennial plants, unique hanging baskets, and unusual trees and shrubs.

INTRODUCTION

OUTDOOR MUSEUMS

The Smithsonian experience does not begin and end at the doors of its museums. Beyond the museum walls are gardens and interior courtyards that have been designed to augment and complement the collections within. Taken together, the Smithsonian gardens (most of them on the National Mall) create a *bona fide* botanic garden. As with the metamorphosis of the institution itself, the growth of its gardens was often the result of pure serendipity.

In 1791, at the behest of President George Washington, the French military engineer and architect Pierre Charles L'Enfant (1754–1825) set out to plan the future capital of the United States. He was able to see beyond the rough, poorly drained farmland around him and envision an elegant and ambitious design. The plan he drew is reminiscent of the layout of Versailles, in which *allées* radiate from the center of absolute power, the chambers of King Louis XIV.

In the Washington plan, the streets and boulevards were planned to emanate from the symbol of democracy, the U.S. Capitol. The dominant feature of L'Enfant's design was to be a grand avenue stretching from the Capitol to a statue of George Washington, lined with important buildings and crowned by gardens. During the century that followed its creation, however, only gradual progress was made toward the fulfillment of L'Enfant's plan. It was too grandiose, too expensive, and too far ahead of its time for the young, struggling democracy to implement.

In 1791, when most of Washington, D.C., was a swampy wilderness, Pierre L'Enfant envisioned an elegant city. Not surprising for a plan by an eighteenth-century Frenchman, the main boulevards he designed emanated from the seat of democracy, the U.S. Capitol. This feature is reminiscent of Versailles, where allées radiate from the palace of Louis XIV.

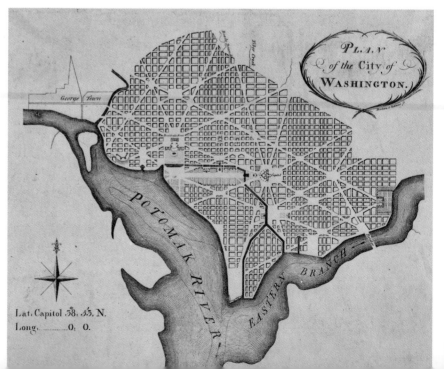

In 1835, out of the blue, the United States government was notified that the British scientist James Smithson (ca. 1765–1829) had left his estate to "the people of the United States of America" to establish an institution in his name "for the increase and diffusion of knowledge." Two decades after the end of the War of 1812, a bequest from an unknown British citizen with aristocratic ties who had never set foot in the United States met with varying reactions. Many were befuddled, some were pleased, but a few were angered and argued against accepting it. Nevertheless, on August 28, 1838, when the packet ship *Mediator*, a swift mail boat, docked in New York Harbor, it carried the American diplomat Richard Rush, accompanied by Smithson's legacy: 105 sacks of gold sovereigns.

Once the money was in hand, Smithson's somewhat vague mandate, "for the increase and diffusion of knowledge," engendered endless interpretation and haggling. Former President John Quincy Adams wanted to use the funds to establish a national observatory. The diplomat and South Carolina congressman Joel Poinsett favored his National Institute for the Promotion of Sciences as a recipient of the legacy. Others backed proposals for a school, a library, or a female academy.

The ideas were still being hotly debated in 1842, when Charles Dickens (1812–70) made his first visit to the United States. The famous author's stingingly accurate words in *American Notes* (1842) portrayed Washington as a place of lofty but unfulfilled aspirations. He called it the "City of Magnificent Intentions." Only from the top of the Capitol, he wrote, could one comprehend the "aspiring Frenchman" L'Enfant's design. Dickens disparaged the few features of L'Enfant's plan that had been realized, calling them "spacious avenues, that begin in nothing, and lead nowhere." He found no gardens, only "waste ground with frowzy grass."

The Smithsonian Institution's British benefactor, James Smithson, never visited America. His unexpected bequest stunned, pleased, and bewildered members of the young American government. Secretary Joseph Henry urged in 1846 that Smithson's name not be "transmitted to posterity by a monument of brick and mortar, but by the effects of his institution on his fellow men."

The founding of the Smithsonian Institution marked a turning point for those magnificent intentions and the beginning of the Mall's development. Among the designs submitted to house the institution was one by the architect Robert Mills (1781–1855), who designed the U.S. Department of the Treasury (1839) and Patent Office (1836–68) Buildings. His plan for a romantic, medieval-style edifice was accompanied by a design for the entire Mall that included a botanic garden. Ultimately the building committee of the Board of Regents selected a design by James Renwick Jr. (1818–95) for a Romanesque Revival–style structure. Its towers and chimneys recalled the rooflines of the Old World's universities and associated this building with a tradition of learning and knowledge. The towers also gave rise to the Smithsonian building's nickname, the "Castle."

The garden on the Castle's south side (opposite) is inviting in any season. In the winter, snow "flowers" cling to the leafless branches of a saucer magnolia (Magnolia × soulangeana).

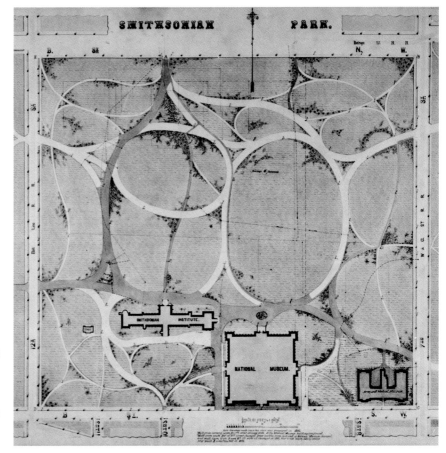

Although the landscape designer Andrew Jackson Downing died in 1852, a plan developed some thirty years later for the "Smithsonian Park" nonetheless reflected his influence. It depicts curvilinear walks and carriage drives of the kind that Downing had intended for a park that would be "a public museum of living trees and shrubs."

With an impressive new building under construction, President Millard Fillmore turned his attention to development of the grounds. To design a landscape plan for the Mall area, he commissioned America's most prominent horticulturist and landscape designer, Andrew Jackson Downing (1815–52). A proponent of the natural style of gardening, Downing—who believed wholeheartedly in the civilizing effects of beauty in landscapes—dismissed L'Enfant's plan, probably finding it elitist as well as too formal. In place of a grand avenue, Downing proposed four parks that would create "a public museum of living trees and shrubs." These parks would be interconnected with curvilinear walks and carriage drives.

Downing's picturesque plan was begun in 1851. Photographs in the Smithsonian Institution Archives taken in the late nineteenth and early twentieth centuries show copses of mature trees, a busy market, and carriage drives on the Mall. After Downing died in a steamboat accident in 1852, his plan was not completed. Further efforts to develop the Mall were shelved during the Civil War. The army used the Mall to bivouac and parade, and railroad tracks cut across part of its south side.

It was not until 1902 that the McMillan Commission—a group of preeminent architects, landscape architects, urban planners, and the noted sculptor Augustus Saint-Gaudens, chaired by Michigan Senator James McMillan—submitted a plan to Congress that purported to restore L'Enfant's concept for the Mall. Instead of a grand avenue, there would be a great lawn. It would extend from the Capitol to the Washington Monument, which had been completed in 1884. Four rows of American elm trees (*Ulmus americana*) would flank the Mall, beyond which would be public buildings. To implement the plan, thousands of trees, greenhouses of the United States Botanic Garden, monuments, ponds, gardens, residences, and a railway station had to be moved or demolished to make way for a level greensward and orderly rows of elms. Despite public outcry, the McMillan Plan prevailed, but the final clearing of the Mall was not concluded until the 1930s.

Meanwhile the Smithsonian expanded its presence on the Mall, museum by museum. In 1902 two Smithsonian buildings were there. The Castle, completed in 1855, contained a museum, a library, a gallery of art, lecture halls, and laboratories, as well as residential quarters for the family of Joseph Henry (1797–1878), the first Smithsonian secretary, and for Smithsonian naturalists. Display space within the Castle was severely limited, and Henry narrowly interpreted the mandate, "for the increase and diffusion of knowledge." He considered the Smithsonian to be a research institution concerned primarily with the receipt and distribution of scientific publications, not with exhibits to edify or entertain the public.

From Independence Avenue, the Renwick Gates open to the south side of the Castle and the Enid A. Haupt Garden, noted for its central parterre. Completing the Quadrangle are the Arthur M. Sackler Gallery on the left and the National Museum of African Art on the right.

Spencer Fullerton Baird (1823–87), Henry's assistant secretary, was a born collector who had a breadth of scientific interests—and a big dream. He wanted a national museum that would showcase precisely the kinds of exhibits that Henry disdained. At the close of the Centennial Exhibition in Philadelphia in 1876, Baird talked representatives from thirty-four countries and several states into donating their fair exhibits to the Smithsonian. He returned to Washington with sixty boxcars full of artifacts that would become the nucleus of the National Museum, housed in a polychrome Victorian building designed by Adolf Cluss (1825–1905) and Paul Schulze (1827–97) and completed in 1881. The construction of what is today known as the Arts and Industries Building signaled a new direction for Smithson's mandate. It was the beginning of the Smithsonian's democratization: henceforth the institution would include both research and public sides.

Twenty years later, the National Museum of Natural History was built on the Mall's north side. It was followed in 1923 by the opening of the Freer Gallery of Art, with its contemplative courtyard garden. Together with the Castle, the Arts and Industries Building, and Independence Avenue, the Freer formed the fourth side of a rectangle, known as the South Yard and later as the Quadrangle. This space, where endangered bison grazed in the 1880s, would eventually welcome the Enid A. Haupt Garden. While space for the bison and other wildlife was found at the institution's new 170-acre National Zoological Park in Northwest Washington, Smithsonian museums became the dominant presence on the Mall. More were to come.

In 1964 the Museum of History and Technology (later renamed the National Museum of American History) opened to the public. In 1968, not far from the Mall, the National Portrait Gallery and the American Art Museum opened in the Patent Office Building, constructed around an interior garden courtyard. In 1974 the Hirshhorn Museum and Sculpture Garden was built next to the Arts and Industries Building. Two years later, on July 1, 1976, the National Air and Space Museum opened in time for the American Bicentennial festivities. When the National Museum of the American Indian was launched in 2004, it brought the total of highly maintained garden space around the Smithsonian's museums to more than twenty-eight acres. Today these areas provide the finishing touches to development of the Mall, a process two centuries in the making.

A bird's-eye view shows the walled, sunken Hirshhorn Sculpture Garden and, directly across the Mall, the National Gallery of Art's Sculpture Garden.

In stark contrast to more traditional landscaping in the nation's capital, the landscape of the National Museum of the American Indian (opposite) is a beautiful blend of native wildflowers, shrubs, and trees.

The Office of Horticulture

S. Dillon Ripley (1913–2001), the eighth secretary of the Smithsonian, recognized a golden opportunity in the landscapes around the museums. Remembering the museums and European pleasure gardens he had visited in his youth, he was determined to develop surroundings for the Smithsonian museums that would be as remarkable as their interiors. To turn mundane grounds into display gardens and ultimately to establish horticulture as a part of the institution's research and education efforts, Ripley created the Office of Horticulture in 1972. Its first director, James R. Buckler, was a visionary who was blessed with a can-do assistant director, Jack Monday, and a capable staff that embarked on the greening of the Smithsonian.

Working behind the scenes, the Greenhouse Nursery Operations branch is responsible for the greening of the Smithsonian. Tropical plants destined for horticultural displays inside and outside the Smithsonian museums are tended in one of the new state-of-the-art greenhouses.

In preparation for America's Bicentennial in 1976, one of the Office of Horticulture's first efforts was a Victorian parterre, modeled after an example in *Henderson's Picturesque Gardens and Ornamental Gardening* (1884). The extravagant Victorian Garden was the popular forerunner of the parterre in the Haupt Garden. In conjunction with the parterre display, Buckler acquired Victorian furniture and other artifacts, which became the nucleus of what is now the Garden Furnishings and Horticultural Artifacts Collections.

At first the Office of Horticulture was housed in a Quonset hut in the South Yard, along with a greenhouse in which employees propagated bedding materials and exotic species. As plans to renovate existing gardens and add new ones mushroomed, the available greenhouse space on the Mall was quickly rendered inadequate. Greenhouses on the historic grounds of the Armed Forces Retirement Home were leased in 1975. Soon tropical plants began to adorn the museums' interiors. Lawn areas around the museums gave way to masses of flowers, and vacant spaces sprouted gardens. The unit burgeoned into three interrelated branches, each with its own manifold responsibilities: Grounds Management Operations, Greenhouse Nursery Operations, and Horticulture Collections Management and Education.

The establishment of the Office of Horticulture coincided with a great boom in gardening in the United States that began in the 1970s. By 1986 a Gallup Poll listed gardening as the number one outdoor activity in American households, ahead of golf, jogging, boating, tennis, and swimming. Horticulture at the Smithsonian grew in tandem with the surging interest around the country.

On entering the Arthur M. Sackler Gallery, visitors are greeted with a resplendent floral arrangement by the horticulturist Cheyenne Kim. In 1997 Else Sackler, the wife of the museum's benefactor, established an endowment to support a floral display that is renewed each week.

SMITHSONIAN GARDENS

Buoyed by the immense popularity of gardening, which spawned interest in everything from vegetables to native plants, the Smithsonian began to regard its growing roster of gardens collectively as a single botanic garden, one that is educational as well as ornamental. By 2010, when the Horticulture Services Division (successor to the Office of Horticulture) was renamed Smithsonian Gardens, its mission had also been further refined: to enrich the Smithsonian experience through exceptional gardens, horticultural exhibits, collections, and education. Not only the gardens outside, but numerous exhibitions within the walls of the museums are also informed by plants from Smithsonian Gardens's extensive collections and collaborations between horticulturists and curators.

At the Smithsonian American Art Museum and the National Portrait Gallery, the canopy over the Robert and Arlene Kogod Courtyard holds 864 panes of blown glass from Poland, of which no two are alike. The canopy keeps this hidden retreat warm and dry year-round.

As individual as the museums they enhance, the gardens of the Smithsonian are wonderfully varied. The exuberant plantings of the Mary Livingston Ripley Garden testify to the enormous range of ornamental plants available today, a happy result of the gardening boom. A stroll on a summer day through this garden, located between the Arts and Industries Building and the Hirshhorn Museum and Sculpture Garden, presents dozens of refreshing combinations of herbaceous and woody, temperate and tropical plants. The Heirloom and Victory Gardens at the National Museum of American History arise from a distinctly American past and mirror the nation's Zeitgeist at different times in its history. The Heirloom Garden is nostalgic, filled with the homey flowers cherished in simpler times. The Victory Garden commemorates the patriotic, communal spirit at home while World War II was fought half a world away.

From the more recent past, the Butterfly Habitat Garden at the National Museum of Natural History reflects a better understanding of processes in the natural world, while the terrace garden at the National Air and Space Museum is an eco-smart response to local growing conditions. The contemporary works in the Hirshhorn Sculpture Garden are enhanced by complementary plantings that serve as transcendent gallery walls. The Kogod Courtyard at the Donald W. Reynolds Center for American Art and Portraiture offers an urban retreat under an overhead canopy that is a triumph of modern technology.

Winding between the Mall and Independence Avenue, the brick paths in the Mary Livingston Ripley Garden (opposite) wander through richly planted garden beds and quiet alcoves. A sliver of the Hirshhorn Sculpture Garden can be seen in the distance.

Other Smithsonian gardens are reminiscent of Old World models. The Freer
Courtyard was inspired by the medieval courtyards that Charles Lang Freer
visited on his travels in Britain. The Haupt Garden's parterre derives from a
seventeenth- and eighteenth-century French garden style that spread throughout
Europe, died out, was revived in Victorian England, and became a popular
exhibit at the 1876 Philadelphia Centennial Exhibition. The Kathrine Dulin
Folger Rose Garden is a timeless classic that might as likely be found on the
grounds of an ancient monastery as on the National Mall.

Some gardens break with Western gardening prototypes. The Moongate Garden
at the Arthur M. Sackler Gallery honors the traditions of Asia, while the
Fountain Garden at the National Museum of African Art incorporates conven-
tions from Islam's long history. The landscape surrounding the National
Museum of the American Indian harkens back four hundred years to a time
before there was a European presence in America and uses the region's raw
materials to create a uniquely contemporary garden.

Still other gardens farther from the Mall offer respite from urban settings. The
National Zoological Park in Northwest Washington, D.C., presents thousands of
plants and animals in a natural environment in order to communicate the impor-

tance of nature to the welfare of both people and animals. The Arthur Ross Terrace and Garden at the Cooper-Hewitt, National Design Museum offers access to what was once one of Manhattan's largest private gardens.

Despite the wide diversity of the Smithsonian gardens, all benefit from environmentally sensitive practices that horticulturists employ each and every day. Handsome natives grow in most of the gardens. Landscaping with native or climatically suitable plants provides an environmentally appropriate and arresting alternative to traditional landscaping. In a similar vein, Smithsonian Gardens practices integrated pest management as a way of controlling garden pests using methods that are the least hazardous to people and the environment. These are just a few of the countless elements in the Smithsonian gardens that inspire and set examples for visitors from all over the world.

Carefully planned to advance the mission and enhance the experience of the museum it surrounds, each of the Smithsonian gardens is distinctive and ever evolving. Most are situated along the Mall, a prominent feature in a plan that was executed when the city of Washington was little more than a magnificent intention. All together, these Smithsonian gardens compose a living history of gardening in America.

Thundering down a wall of rough stone, the waterfall at Lemur Island is a popular part of the Smithsonian's National Zoo, located in Rock Creek Park.

ENID A. HAUPT GARDEN

Andrew Jackson Downing quickly rose to become America's foremost landscape designer during his short professional career. Just thirty-seven years old, he died in 1852 in a steamboat accident at the height of his career.

James Renwick Jr. designed the Smithsonian's first building with towers, turrets, and chimneys that call to mind universities of the Old World. Although the south side of the Castle was left as open space, this 1858 photograph shows that its north entrance was wreathed in a romantic carpet of wildflowers.

The intricate parterre on the Castle's south side (opposite), enhanced by rows of saucer magnolias (Magnolia × soulangeana), is the heart of the Enid A. Haupt Garden.

On May 22, 1987, the day the Enid A. Haupt Garden opened to the public, eager visitors entered, stopped, and gazed in awe. Spread out before them was a fully mature garden. A central parterre blazing with hundreds of pansies was flanked by *allées* of twenty-foot-tall pink saucer magnolias (*Magnolia × soulangiana*). A pair of tall ginkgos (*Ginkgo biloba*) framed the Castle's south entrance, and a giant European linden (*Tilia europaea*) dominated the northeast corner.

One question loomed. How was it possible that this garden—on a rooftop, no less—had grown to this extraordinary fullness when just four short years earlier it had been a giant hole in the ground?

Although this garden had not enjoyed the luxury of gradual growth, the notion of green space on the Castle's south side harkened back to the original plan. In the 1840s, when the architect James Renwick Jr. (1818–95) designed the Smithsonian's first building, he placed the main entrance on the Mall side and intentionally left the area behind the Castle as green space. At the time, acres of open land stretched all the way to the Potomac River. A later plan for the Mall by the landscape designer and horticulturist Andrew Jackson Downing (1815–52), drawn around 1850 but never fully implemented, similarly addressed mainly the Castle's north side.

THE DOWNING URN

The Downing Urn occupies the place where the European linden (Tilia europaea) once stood (see sidebar, page 35). In a circular garden that is shaded by three little-leaf lindens (Tilia cordata 'June Bride'), the urn commemorates the man who was considered America's foremost landscape designer, Andrew Jackson Downing (1815–52). He died at the height of his career in a steamboat accident before a plan he developed for the National Mall was fully implemented.

The marble urn, dedicated by the American Pomological Society, was designed by Downing's business partner, Calvert Vaux (1824–95), who, with Frederick Law Olmsted (1822–1903), later designed New York's Central Park. On the grounds of the Smithsonian since 1856, the badly deteriorated Downing Urn was restored in 1972 and was moved to its present location in 1989. On one side of the pedestal supporting the Downing Urn is the following passage from Downing's Rural Essays (1853):

Plant spacious parks in your cities,
and unclose their gates as wide
as the gates of morning to the whole people

Because the building served as home to the Smithsonian's first secretary, the physicist Joseph Henry (1797–1878), and his family, it is probable that the yard's initial use was private. But in an era when Washington was growing rapidly, open land close to the city center did not stay undeveloped. Soon a railroad and a street ran between the Castle and the river. The space immediately behind the Castle, by then identified as the South Yard, was soon pressed into service. For the next century, the South Yard served the changing needs of the Smithsonian. Historic photographs document it in a series of incarnations. One, taken in the 1880s, shows a taxidermy shop in a building identified as "the South Shed."

The South Shed in the South Yard, seen in the early 1900s, stood directly behind the Castle. Built in 1898, it was torn down in the fall of 1975 in preparation for the Victorian Garden, which opened in 1976.

Taxidermy was one of many industries undertaken in the South Yard. Pictured in the 1880s in the South Shed, William Temple Hornaday (center), a taxidermist and zookeeper, works on a tiger to be mounted for exhibit.

29

Among the taxidermists and hunters working for the Smithsonian was William Temple Hornaday (1854–1937), who traveled to eastern Montana for bison specimens. After witnessing the shocking extermination of large herds of bison, the erstwhile hunter swiftly turned conservationist. Writing in 1887 to Professor George Brown Goode, the Smithsonian's assistant secretary, Hornaday urged that bison be protected before they became extinct: "It is the general belief," he wrote and emphasized, "that *not over twenty head remain.*"

To address this plea, the South Yard was transformed into a zoo with bison penned in a paddock. This popular attraction helped excite public interest and support for the conservation of these endangered animals. In 1889 Congress passed an act founding the National Zoological Park. To the satisfaction of neighbors who complained of the smell, the bison were moved to the zoo, a place that third Secretary Samuel P. Langley (1834–1906) described as "a refuge for vanishing races of the continent."

Before the National Zoological Park was established in 1889, bison were penned in the Castle's South Yard. This preservation measure was urged by William Temple Hornaday, who also wrote The Extermination of the American Bison *as a call to action.*

In the same year, in a letter to the Smithsonian's Board of Regents, Langley made a modest request. The astronomer and astrophysicist asked for "a wooden structure of the simplest and most temporary character" for use as an astrophysical laboratory. The building erected for the Aerodrome Shop was subsequently enlarged, with additions of three smaller structures made between 1893 and 1898. A succession of buildings was to populate the South Yard, including a solar radiation lab and a "bug house," where industrious beetles did the work of cleaning the skeletal remains of animal specimens. Many were used as temporary storage and preparation areas for collections.

Yet another outbuilding in the South Yard was a hangar, built by the U.S. Army in 1917. It was transferred to the Smithsonian at the end of World War I, after which it housed a growing collection of planes, missiles, and rockets. Missiles and rockets too large to fit in the hangar simply stood in what came to be called Rocket Row in the South Yard. Eventually the collection was moved to the National Air and Space Museum, which opened in 1976.

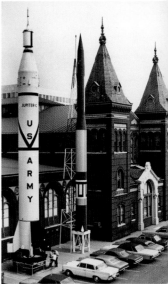

In 1972 the South Yard began a return to green space. The Office of Horticulture, under the management of Director James R. Buckler, came into being as a museum program. The South Yard housed the Office of Horticulture in a Quonset hut and a greenhouse in which employees propagated bedding materials and exotic plant species. For the celebration of America's Bicentennial in 1976, bedding plants—thousands of them—were just what was needed. The Office of Horticulture created a Victorian Garden in the South Yard to augment an exhibition of Victoriana in the Arts and Industries Building next door.

That exhibition displayed artifacts from sixty boxcars of material that had been donated to the Smithsonian one hundred years earlier, after the 1876 Centennial Exhibition in Philadelphia closed. To complement this exhibition, the Victorian Garden featured a parterre in the center of the South Yard patterned after the sunken garden designed for the Centennial. Victorian urns and benches arranged throughout the garden elaborated on the theme. While the exhibition in the Arts and Industries Building entertained visitors, the Victorian Garden in the South Yard captured their hearts. Visitors strolled through the garden, rested on its ornate benches, listened to water splashing in its fountain, and fell in love with this lush 2.8-acre oasis in the busy city.

The Victorian Garden was intended to be temporary, but the public had become fond of it. When plans were announced to remove it during the construction of the underground Quadrangle museum complex, voices were raised in protest. S. Dillon Ripley (1913–2001), the eighth secretary of the Smithsonian, took the brunt of the criticism but stood his ground and worked toward implementing a grand vision. His dream that the Smithsonian Institution expand its horizons beyond Western culture would find fulfillment in the addition of museums there to showcase Asian and African art.

From late spring into fall, plants in containers—including specimen palms—transform the west side of the Arts and Industries Building into a tropical garden. They surround Leonard Baskin's bronze statue (1975–77) of Spencer Fullerton Baird, the Smithsonian's second secretary.

Once a utilitarian service area, the South Yard has been transformed into the stunning Haupt Garden (opposite). The Downing Urn, a tribute to the great landscape designer, rises above a meadow of coneflowers (Echinacea sp. and Echinacea × hybrida) and ornamental grasses.

33

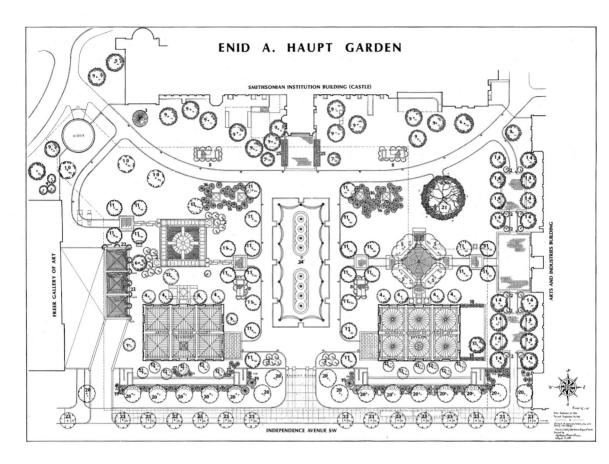

SMITHSONIAN INSTITUTION BUILDING (CASTLE)

KIOSK

FREER GALLERY OF ART

ARTS AND INDUSTRIES BUILDING

INDEPENDENCE AVENUE SW

Although situated at ground level, the Haupt Garden is actually a rooftop garden placed directly atop a massive underground museum complex. The elaborate parterre, at the center; the Moongate Garden, at the left; and the Fountain Garden, at the right, complement the architecture of the museums they adjoin.

In 1979 President Jimmy Carter signed a bill authorizing the appropriation of $500,000 for the planning of the South Quadrangle Project. What had once been called the South Yard and later the Victorian Garden was now referred to as the Quadrangle complex because the new construction would take place within a quadrangle bordered by the Castle, the Freer Gallery of Art, the Arts and Industries Building, and Independence Avenue. The Quadrangle complex centered on the addition of three new Smithsonian museum spaces: the Arthur M. Sackler Gallery, displaying Asian antiquities; the National Museum of African Art, exhibiting works from Sub-Saharan Africa expanded from a private collection amassed by Warren M. Robbins; and the International Center, now the S. Dillon Ripley Center, containing exhibit galleries, offices, classrooms, and an auditorium.

Under the best circumstances, the design and construction of a vast, 4.2-acre museum complex within feet of the venerable Castle, Freer Gallery, and Arts and Industries Building would be inordinately challenging. What made it all the more formidable was that 96 percent of the Quadrangle complex would be underground. On its roof, at street level, was to be a garden.

THE EUROPEAN LINDEN TREE

For as long as anyone could remember, a majestic European linden tree (*Tilia europaea*) dominated the northeast corner of the South Yard. Casting cooling shade in the summer, the linden was beloved by all who knew it, including Secretary S. Dillon Ripley. When construction began on the Quadrangle complex, Ripley's mandate to the design team was to spare the tree.

To do so, the 360,000-square-foot underground complex was actually built around the linden. During construction, from 1983 to 1987, a team of arborists and plant pathologists pruned, fed, and strung cables on the linden to protect its limbs. The tree was fitted with a lightning rod and surrounded by a fence as safekeeping from construction vehicles. A sprinkler system washed construction dust from its leaves.

The linden tree, visible between the Castle and the Arts and Industries Building, survived the Quadrangle's construction. A few years later, in 1989—despite heroic efforts—the aged tree died.

Despite this extraordinary care, the declining tree succumbed to old age. On the afternoon of January 4, 1989, to the dismay of all, the linden toppled to the ground.

From the outset, the garden was integral to the design of the Quadrangle. The principal architect, Jean Paul Carlhian of the Boston firm Shepley, Bulfinch, Richardson, and Abbott, collaborated on the project with Sasaki Associates, Inc., of Watertown, Massachusetts, and the New York landscape architect Lester Collins (1914–93). In preparation for construction, the Victorian Garden was removed in 1982. Groundbreaking for the Quadrangle complex took place on June 21, 1983.

Although there was never any doubt that a new Victorian Garden would replace its cherished predecessor, the space above the museum complex was a third larger than the previous garden. It was clear that the area offered more garden space than what was necessary for a central Victorian parterre. Secretary Ripley considered this bonus space and entertained the idea of adding a Zen garden, one that would be in keeping with a museum housing Asian art and serve as a quiet retreat from the often bustling Mall. He hoped to interest the publishing heiress and philanthropist Enid A. Haupt (1906–2005) in financing it.

The philanthropist Enid A. Haupt, to the left of Lady Bird Johnson, financed and endowed the garden over the Smithsonian's Quadrangle complex that bears her name.

Ripley had good reason to hope. If ever there were a fairy godmother for American horticulture, it was Enid Haupt. She had purchased River Farm in Alexandria, Virginia, once owned by George Washington, and donated it to the American Horticultural Society. She had underwritten the Haupt Fountains on the Ellipse between the White House and the Washington Monument; endowed the Enid A. Haupt Glass Garden, a therapeutic space at the New York University Medical Center; and contributed to the renovation and endowment of the conservatory at the New York Botanical Garden. To finance her generous donations, she had been known to sell off paintings and jewelry. Her religion, she often said, was nature.

The saucer magnolias (Magnolia × soulangeana) in the Haupt Garden are stunning when they bloom in the spring (right and opposite). They are beautiful even in the winter, when their trunks resemble sinewy, silvery sculpture.

Haupt was invited to tour the garden site with Secretary Ripley, architect Carlhian, and others who hoped to interest her in a Zen garden. After the tour she announced that she was not interested in underwriting a Zen garden. The dismay of those present was profound but only momentary. "I'm only interested in financing the whole thing," she is reported to have said. "The entire garden. How much do you think it will cost?"

For the design and construction of the Enid A. Haupt Garden, Haupt pledged an endowment of $3 million. With such generous financing in place, the realization of a new garden was ensured, but its actualization would not be accomplished without great effort. In her late seventies at the time, the benefactor did not want to wait for the garden to mature. She stipulated that it be mature when it opened. That was a demanding requirement, but an even greater challenge overshadowed all others: the garden not only had to advance the themes of the Sackler and African Art museums, it also had to harmonize the varied surrounding buildings.

The three existing museums that flanked the garden site had been constructed in different eras, in different architectural styles, and from different materials. The Romanesque Revival Castle (1847–55) was composed of red sandstone. The Freer Gallery (1917–23) was built with granite and marble in the Italian Renaissance style. And the polychrome Victorian style of the Arts and Industries Building (1879–81) featured geometric brick patterns. Along with these buildings, pavilions denoting the underground museums as well as an entry kiosk were to rise into the garden like the tips of icebergs, adding yet other architectural styles.

Riveting red, these tulips (Tulipa 'Bastogne') are some of the thousands that brighten the Smithsonian gardens in the spring.

Majestic when flanked by tropical plants, the Downing Urn (opposite) is bordered by palms and purple leaf crinums (Crinum augustum 'Queen Emma') in a ground cover of foxtail ferns (Asparagus densiflorus 'Meyersii') and yellow Joseph's coat (Alternanthera ficoidea 'True Yellow').

Containers of tropical Heliconia line a shady path that leads to the Fountain Garden. Brick walkways connect the Arts and Industries Building and the Castle and harmonize with their brick and red sandstone materials.

In addition to a new central parterre to replace the Victorian Garden, Carlhian added a Moongate Garden adjacent to the Sackler Gallery and a Fountain Garden next to the African Art Museum. To link all the buildings with these three distinct parts of the garden, the architect first established two axes that meet in the very heart of the parterre. The first, a strong north-south axis, extends from the Castle's south door to the Renwick Gates on Independence Avenue. The broad parterre that spans most of its length powerfully reinforces this axis. The other axis begins from east to west along a path that is inset with bricks, echoing the color of the Castle and the Arts and Industries Building. It enters the Sackler Gallery's Moongate Garden along its northern edge but pinwheels around the garden to exit in line with the garden's southern edge. This neat trick allows the axis to continue through the exact center of the parterre. It moves directly

It took more than a century to realize James Renwick's 1849 design for entrance gates to the Smithsonian. Constructed in 1979 of wrought and cast iron, the gates on Independence Avenue are mounted on four massive pillars, composed of the same red sandstone as the Castle. James Goode, keeper of the Castle, found much of the sandstone at a closed quarry in Seneca, Maryland. The piers were carved by the master stone carver Constantine Seferlis, who spent years working on the National Cathedral in Washington.

through the middle of the African Art pavilion's Fountain Garden and culminates in the center of the Arts and Industries Building. The axes underlay the garden, lending it symmetry and a snug sense of structure. They bring the Quadrangle's varied elements into harmony.

For motifs, Carlhian studied the existing buildings to find common elements that might be carried into the new museum complex and garden. He extracted patterns such as a diamond from the sharply angled rooflines of the Arts and Industries Building and a circle from the rounded arches over windows and entrances of the Freer Gallery and the Castle. The diamond and the circle became leitmotifs that figure inside and outside the new museums and in the garden. The copper roof composed of six pointed pyramids that tops the Sackler pavilion is echoed in the diamond shape of the Fountain Garden. The circular openings in the gates and the island in the Moongate Garden repeat the shape of the six circular copper domes on the African Art pavilion.

A place where the two motifs come together is the kiosk that serves as the entrance to the S. Dillon Ripley Center. Its domed roof is edged with scallops that combine the diamond and the circle motifs. Located on the garden's Mall side, the kiosk is a playful structure reminiscent of a bandstand on a village green. Even though its appearance is whimsical, its purpose as a gateway to the Ripley Center three stories below is crucial.

Edged with scallops and located behind a bright fringe of shrimp plant (Pachystachys lutea), the S. Dillon Ripley Center's domed roof is reminiscent of a bandstand on a village green.

Designs in the Haupt Garden's parterre can change from year to year as well as from season to season. Diamond shapes, fleurs-de-lis, and scallops or swags are some of the variations used.

As the largest element in the Quadrangle, the stunning parterre is the bold heart of the Enid A. Haupt Garden. The axes that tie together the garden meet precisely in its center, while its generous dimensions are in keeping with the massive buildings around it. Low-growing plants are carefully manicured to form the symmetrical parterre design, which is variously a series of diamonds, *fleurs-de-lis*, scallops, or swags as the plants change with the seasons. Typically in winter, pansies are the workhorses, bringing color to the design. In spring these winter stalwarts are exchanged for tulips and colorful annuals that have been nurtured in the Smithsonian greenhouses.

Taking advantage of Washington's long growing season, a splendid collection of tropicals, including bananas that winter in the Smithsonian greenhouses, spend the warm months enhancing the space along the west side of the Arts and Industries Building. Beside the Castle's south face, a richly varied collection of unusual evergreens and deciduous plants thrive in the sheltered warmth of the garden. Among these plants is the Wollemi pine (*Wollemia nobilis*), one of the world's oldest and rarest conifers, only about a hundred specimens of which exist in the wild.

The Parterre

The word *parterre* is thought to be either from the French *par terre* ("on the ground") or from the Italian *partire* ("to divide"). Both words describe the way that low-growing flowers, foliage plants, and shrubs are carefully positioned within a flower bed to form blocks of color in elaborate patterns. The effect of a parterre is that of a colorful flower carpet.

The parterre in the Enid A. Haupt Garden measures 144 feet long by 66 feet wide. Plants that make up the parterre's design are grown in the Smithsonian greenhouses and are changed every six months, usually in September and May. Replanting, which takes a day or two, occurs after meticulous measuring by Smithsonian Gardens horticulturists to ensure that the planting layout is symmetrical.

The parterre in the Haupt Garden replaced the popular Victorian Garden, which was removed when the Quadrangle was developed.

THE MOONGATE GARDEN

Jean Paul Carlhian, designer of the Moongate Garden adjacent to the Sackler
Gallery, found inspiration for it in the Temple of Heaven in Beijing. The
Moongate Garden similarly possesses a timeless quality that derives from the
logic and utter simplicity of its design. Its essential components are water and
stone. In Chinese culture these elements symbolize the spirit and the body of the
earth. Here they figure in a layout that is at once archaic and modern: a circle
within a square that is aligned with the cardinal points of the compass.

Circles, a motif borrowed from the African Art pavilion, figure prominently in
this garden. Circular openings in massive nine-foot blocks of pink granite
provide monumental entrances. These circular openings follow the classic
Chinese convention of gates that frame views at the same time they powerfully
set up and direct an east-west axis through the garden. In the northeast and
southwest corners of the Moongate Garden, two more colossal granite blocks lie
on their sides. Built from the same pink material as the entrances, these function
as stone benches, providing seating with a tranquil view of the central pool. In
the center of the square is a shallow pool with a circular island accessed by four
bridges. The bottom of the pool is paved with lustrous black granite that contrasts smartly with the pink granite island and renders an illusion of depth.

In keeping with the garden's simple lines, the planting is restrained. Hedges
of boxwood (Buxus sp.) and ground covers of lily turf (Liriope sp.) and dwarf mondo
grass (Ophiopogon muscari japonicus) provide evergreen shelter and texture. Azaleas
and a weeping Higan cherry (Prunus × subhirtella var. pendula) bring spring color.

The Fountain Garden

Adjacent to the National Museum of African Art, the Fountain Garden was inspired by the Lion Court in the Alhambra Palace in Granada, Spain. Built in the thirteenth and fourteenth centuries by Moors who crossed from North Africa to Andalusia, the Alhambra is considered an outstanding example of Islamic architecture. The Fountain Garden borrows from the Islamic tradition of the paradise garden, typically a walled rectangle cut by four water channels that cross in the center and divide the garden into quarters. It departs from tradition in that the rectangle has been squared off and turned to create a diamond shape, and the water channels flow along the top of low stone walls on the garden's edges.

In true Islamic tradition, the soul of the Fountain Garden is water. Twelve jets send water coursing through channels in the low walls to cool the air, a welcome feature during Washington's sultry summers. In the center of the garden, a single jet shoots water eight feet in the air. The garden's *chadar* (a stone ramp that slopes to form a waterfall) is engraved with wave patterns similar to those in the Mughal gardens of Kashmir. In the Himalayas, streams from the foothills are diverted to flow through such gardens: *chadars* move water from terrace to terrace down a slope, cooling the air in the process. Here the *chadar* tumbles water into a shallow pool, its patterns creating attractive ripples as the water flows over them. The feature gives off both cooling mist and the pleasant sound of falling water to muffle street noise.

For more than a century and a half, this space behind the Castle—evolving from the South Yard to the Victorian Garden and then the Quadrangle—has addressed the changing needs and interests of the Smithsonian Institution. Never has it served so beautifully and brilliantly as in its final incarnation, the Enid A. Haupt Garden. A synthesis of garden traditions from around the globe, the Haupt Garden has become a treasured and enormously popular Washington icon. Resplendent and welcoming, it is the outward-facing countenance of the museums around and below it.

Water shoots eight feet into the air from the central jet in the Fountain Garden. Around it, twelve additional jets send cooling water through channels in the walls.

Expansive views of the Haupt Garden, including star-shaped plantings in the parterre (opposite), greet visitors at the pavilion entrance of the National Museum of African Art.

The Fountain Garden includes a chadar (a stone ramp with flowing water), which is a feature borrowed from Mughal gardens. During the summer months, container plants add lushness to the space.

Courtyard

Freer Gallery of Art

The simple logic and the human scale of the Freer Gallery of Art often inspire visitors to remark on its intimate feel. Enhancing this impression is the open courtyard at the heart of the Italian Renaissance–style building. Although more than half a million people visit the Freer each year, its courtyard remains the most private and peaceful of all the Smithsonian gardens. The building and the courtyard are credited to the gallery's designer, Charles A. Platt, but the design evolved slowly, through much thoughtful collaboration with the man who made the museum possible, Charles Lang Freer (1854–1919).

Freer's history is one of those Horatio Alger stories peculiar to the nineteenth century. Despite leaving school after seventh grade, he considerably bettered his fortunes, manufacturing railroad cars and eventually becoming part owner of a railroad. At forty-five he was able to retire from business and dedicate himself full time to acquiring art. A self-taught collector who began his aesthetic education by studying and collecting Japanese prints, he found "points of contact" in them with the art of James McNeill Whistler (1834–1903). Whistler was a close friend who shared the collector's admiration for Chinese and Japanese objects. With Whistler's encouragement, Freer eventually turned his collecting energies from American to Asian art. Between 1894 and 1911, he made several trips to Asia, ultimately acquiring more than 7,500 works from China, Japan, Korea, India, Pakistan, Turkey, Iran, Iraq, Syria, and Central Asia.

Freer offered his collections of Asian and American art—including the world's most important assemblage of Whistler's works—to the Smithsonian in 1904, along with a building in which to display them. At the time the Smithsonian maintained a primarily scientific focus, and the Board of Regents initially turned him down. One reason for the refusal was Freer's insistence on several controversial conditions, including ones that the works never be exhibited outside the museum and that no works be added to or subtracted from the collection. He considered his American collection to be complete but later agreed to allow new works of Asian art to be added to that collection. With encouragement from President Theodore Roosevelt, in 1906 the regents agreed to accept the collections along with a museum building.

Charles Lang Freer donated his collections of American and Asian art to the Smithsonian in 1906 and then turned his attention to envisioning a museum to house them. The idea of having a central courtyard took hold of Freer, an admirer of Italian garden design, on visits to historic buildings abroad.

In the serene Freer Courtyard (opposite), Japanese maples (Acer palmatum 'Burgundy Lace') are a spontaneous and colorful foil to a carefully trimmed evergreen border.

With characteristic discipline, Freer set out to teach himself about museum architecture. Thorough and systematic, he traveled to one after another of Europe's major museums and galleries. The collector deemed the majority "dungeon-like" but found inspiration in medieval buildings in England constructed around interior courtyards.

Arched loggias step down into the Freer Courtyard and frame this secluded space just steps from the bustling Mall. Spokes of marble set into brick pavers radiate out from a fountain and its basin of polished granite.

For the design of his museum, Freer eventually turned to Charles A. Platt (1861–1933), a painter, landscape designer, and prominent proponent of American Renaissance architecture. Both Freer and Platt were great admirers of Italian garden design. As a young art student, Platt had traveled to Italy, where he photographed the refined landscapes that would appear in his popular illustrated book, *Italian Gardens*, published in 1894. Freer was influenced by Platt's preference for the Renaissance style when he began to visualize the design of his gallery. Together Freer and Platt agreed on a building centered around a courtyard that would serve as an outdoor room.

Tolerant of drought, the eight Persian ironwoods (Parrotia persica) in the Freer Courtyard have a graceful spreading habit, brilliant fall color, showy exfoliating bark, and inconspicuous flowers surrounded by ruby red stamens that anticipate the arrival of spring. They are pruned to keep within the confines of the arched frames of the windows overlooking the courtyard.

Ground for the granite and marble building was broken in 1916, but when the United States entered World War I in April 1917, work on the gallery was interrupted and was not completed until late 1919. This construction delay had a tragic consequence: Freer, who had long suffered from the complications of inherited syphilis in the days before the discovery of penicillin, died in September 1919, without seeing his museum finished. Neither did he enjoy its classical courtyard garden, but his gift to the Smithsonian has allowed millions of others to do so since it opened to the public in 1923.

Trained into a rope motif, Japanese boxwoods (Buxus microphylla var. japonica 'Green Beauty') encircle the courtyard's fountain.

Seeking to encourage "contemplation and quiet enjoyment," Freer wanted visitors to see the garden as they moved from gallery to gallery. As a result, all four quadrants of the Freer Gallery open onto an interior courtyard that is elegant in its simplicity. Loggias (covered open-air corridors) provide peaceful and serene settings from which to observe the formal garden. Against the wall of the east loggia are two works in bronze relief by a friend of Platt's, the noted American sculptor Augustus Saint-Gaudens (1848–1907): *Labor Supported by Science and Art* and *Law Supported by Power and Love* (ca. 1894–1900), half-scale models of entrance figures commissioned for the Boston Public Library.

In the courtyard's center is a fountain composed of polished carnelian granite, a dark reddish stone quarried in South Dakota that dates to the Early Proterozoic eon. The fountain rises from a circular basin of the same material, whose color blends with the bricks that pave the courtyard. Strips of white marble radiate through the paving, emphasizing the fountain as the heart of the garden and the museum. (In 1928—before air conditioning was common—some of the paving, at the urging of John E. Lodge, the Freer Gallery's first curator, was replaced with lawn to diminish heat and glare in the galleries.)

In keeping with the museum's classical architecture, the plantings in the courtyard are restrained. Against the north and south sides are eight Persian ironwoods (*Parrotia persica*), uncommon deciduous trees in the witch hazel family from the Alborz Mountains of northern Iran. Four Japanese maples (*Acer palmatum* 'Burgundy Lace') grow on the east and west sides. Around the courtyard, evergreens—cherry laurel (*Prunus laurocerasus*) and Hinoki cypress (*Chamaecyparis obtusa*)—contrast with a trim edging of bright green Japanese boxwood (*Buxus microphylla* var. *japonica* 'Green Beauty'). Circling the central fountain is a neat ring of Japanese boxwoods meticulously trimmed into a rope motif. Bonsai in containers are displayed in the loggias. In warm weather, other containers filled with foliage plants supply seasonal color.

A bonsai juniper in an antique container serves as an understated display on the loggia.

Peacocks were installed temporarily in the Freer Courtyard during the 1920s as a living reference to the gallery's most famous work, James McNeill Whistler's Peacock Room (1876–77). A pair of peacocks made a brief reappearance in the courtyard in the early 1990s.

An extensive renovation of the Freer Gallery, done by Sasaki and Associates, Inc., was begun in 1988. In addition to improvements to the building, the courtyard was dismantled and the four-ton fountain temporarily removed. Two levels were excavated beneath the courtyard to provide expanded space for collections storage. An underground exhibit space was constructed to connect the Freer with the Arthur M. Sackler Gallery, which is located beneath the Quadrangle. Together these galleries form a national museum of Asian art. The courtyard, with plantings devised by the landscape designer Philip Watson of Fredericksburg, Virginia, was repaved in brick as it had been originally. After the project was completed, the courtyard reopened in 1993 with a peacock and a peahen temporarily in residence, as was the practice in the 1920s to complement Whistler's Peacock Room (1876–77) installed inside the museum.

As part of the renovation, the Freer Gallery's front entrance, with its horseshoe-shaped driveway, was redesigned in 1992. The new entrance is more formal to better reflect the building's architecture. A 1981 sculpture by Shiro Hayami made of Agi stone and Peruvian granite, entitled Twisted Form (Traveler's Guardian Spirit), stands in a central circle of lawn and annuals.

Plantings along the pleasant Freer Walk on Twelfth Street between Jefferson Drive and Independence Avenue are deliberately kept simple. Repetition of the colorful bulbs, annuals, and perennials along its length engenders a sense of continuity and classical order appropriate for the Freer building and courtyard.

Twisted Form (Traveler's Guardian Spirit) by Shiro Hayami, from the Hirshhorn Museum and Sculpture Garden's collection, stands outside the Freer Gallery's Mall entrance (opposite). Its surrounding circle of lawn is enhanced by yellow-flowered shrimp plants (Pachystachys lutea) and petunias (Petunia 'Blue Wave').

Kathrine Dulin Folger Rose Garden

Between Smithsonian Castle and Arts and Industries Building

On a snowy winter's day, a walk along the Mall can sometimes yield an unexpected sight—a single rose bloom among the otherwise dormant bushes in the Kathrine Dulin Folger Rose Garden. This delightful sliver of a garden stretches from the east door of the Castle to the entrance of the Arts and Industries Building. It softens the facade of the latter and provides a cozy antechamber to the Enid A. Haupt Garden on the Castle's south side. The Folger is a garden in which to linger and closely examine the roses and their handsome perennial and annual companions. Spacious benches allow for quiet, sheltered seating between the garden and the Arts and Industries Building and, on the Mall side, an opportunity to take in the spectacular view and observe the daily bustle.

Planned to be ornamental in all four seasons, the Folger Rose Garden was dedicated in the fall of 1998. It was made possible by a generous gift from Mr. and Mrs. Lee Merritt Folger to honor Folger's mother, Kathrine Dulin Folger (1904–97) of Washington, D.C., and Palm Beach, Florida. A supporter of horticulture and the Smithsonian, she was the wife of John Clifford Folger, ambassador to Belgium under President Dwight D. Eisenhower. Designed by the landscape architects Paul Lindell and Karen Swanson of Smithsonian Gardens, the present garden replaces a smaller rose garden that dated from the 1970s.

Standouts in the Folger Rose Garden include the hybrid tea rose Rosa 'Opening Night' (above). An antique container (opposite) brims with a colorful mixture of deep purple petunias, lilac verbena, white licorice plant, and Bluebird nemesia.

Even without the happy accident of finding a rogue rose blossom in the snow, the Folger Rose Garden is indeed handsome throughout the year. In winter evergreen shrubs—hollies (*Ilex* × 'Emily Bruner') and boxwoods (*Buxus* sp.)—and winterberries (*Ilex verticillata*) provide color. Early spring brings a burst of bloom, while summer is lush with perennials that complement the roses. The bright yellow foliage of creeping Jenny (*Lysimachia nummularia* 'Aurea') lights up the roses growing over it.

James Alexander Gamble Fragrance Medal Winners

The fragrant hybrid tea rose 'Double Delight' is one of the Gamble Medal winners featured in the Folger Rose Garden. Gamble esteemed fragrance as important a quality in roses as their color, form, and size.

James Alexander Gamble, first president of the Philadelphia Rose Society, examined thousands of roses to determine which were or were not scented. In 1956 he endowed the American Rose Society with funds to award rose hybridizers who produce the finest fragrant roses. Eleven roses in the Kathrine Dulin Folger Rose Garden have won James Alexander Gamble Fragrance Medals for their perfume: 'Crimson Glory' (1961), 'Tiffany' (1962), 'Granada' (1968), 'Fragrant Cloud' (1970), 'Sunsprite' (1979), 'Double Delight' (1986), 'Fragrant Hour' (1997), 'Angel Face' (2001), 'Secret' (2002), 'Mister Lincoln' (2003), and 'Sheila's Perfume' (2005).

Of the many thousands of possible rose candidates, the Folger Rose Garden displays only those classed as modern roses, ones created after 1867. These include hybrid tea, floribunda, grandiflora, shrub, polyantha, miniature, and English roses. In addition, a rose must be of high value and disease resistant. Almost all the roses in the garden have received a rating of 7.0 to 7.9 (good) or 8.0 to 8.9 (excellent) from the All-America Rose Selections, a nonprofit association of rose growers and introducers that rates roses for qualities such as novelty, form, color, fragrance, foliage, and disease resistance. Few roses ever receive a rating of 9.0 (outstanding) or above.

As well as being highly rated, more than two dozen of the roses in the Folger Rose Garden have been AARS or Royal Horticultural Society award winners, chosen as the best of the best in a given year. These include the hybrid teas 'Peace' (AARS, 1946) and 'Mister Lincoln' (AARS, 1965), the grandiflora 'Queen Elizabeth' (AARS, 1955), the floribunda 'French Lace' (AARS, 1982), and the shrub roses 'Knock Out' (AARS, 2000) and 'Golden Celebration' (RHS Award of Garden Merit, 2001).

Visitors whose idea of a good rose is one with a sweet perfume will not be disappointed. In addition to selecting roses on the basis of performance, the horticulturist Shelley Gaskins chose some that have outstanding fragrance. Several roses in the garden are James Alexander Gamble Fragrance Medal winners. The best time to sample their sweet perfume is on the morning of a warm, sunny day, when the scent is strongest. Although hybridizers breed for fragrance, in nature the role of scent is to attract pollinators—chiefly bees. Fragrance will be strongest when the flowers are ready to be pollinated, usually when they are halfway open. Pink or red flowers with thick, velvety petals are likely to have the strongest rose fragrance.

That said, rose fragrance can be fickle and fleeting. A scent that is strong in the first flush of summer bloom may diminish over the course of a season. Scent may also weaken during the day or if a rose bush becomes diseased, especially with mildew. The scent of some roses can even change when a rose is cut and taken inside. And every rose is different, some being more volatile than others. One hybrid tea in the Folger Rose Garden with a stable scent that keeps it smelling like a rose, regardless of conditions, is 'Angel Face.'

All the roses in the Folger Rose Garden are modern (introduced after 1867) and highly rated for ornamental qualities and disease resistance. Shown here are grandiflora R. 'Gold Medal' (below) and floribunda R. 'Angel Face' (bottom).

All modern roses have been hybridized (bred by horticulturists for ornamental qualities). If a rose is deemed outstanding, it is named and introduced to the gardening public. Often stories can be told about the course of their development, their introduction, or their names:

'LA FRANCE,' a pale pink rose with a classic fragrance, is one of the most famous roses of all time, reported to be the first of a new class of rose, the hybrid teas. Created by crossing two types of rose—a hybrid perpetual and a tea rose—a hybrid tea produces a single flower on a long stem that makes it ideal for cut flowers. 'La France' was introduced by Jean-Baptiste Guillot in 1867, making its birth year the dividing line between old and modern roses.

'PEACE,' considered by some rosarians to be one of the finest hybrid teas ever created, dates to the dark days leading to World War II. That's when the French hybridizer Francis Meilland developed a fragrant, disease-resistant rose he called 'Madame A. Meilland.' Its large double blooms were a beautiful blend of yellow and cream. Fearful for the fate of his rose should France be invaded, he sent cuttings to friends in Germany, Italy, Turkey, and the United States. A graft of the rose was also taken out of France in the American consul's suitcase during the war. After the liberation of France, a grateful Meilland wrote to British Field Marshall Alan Brooke, asking permission to name the rose after him. Brooke suggested instead that a better name would be Peace. The rose 'Peace' was introduced in the United States on April 29, 1945, just days before Germany formally surrendered to the Allied Forces on May 8.

The 'ALNWICK ROSE' is a fragrant, double pink English shrub rose developed by David Austin and introduced in 2001. It is named for Alnwick Castle, featured in B.B.C. productions and many films, including the first two *Harry Potter* movies. For more than seven hundred years, Alnwick Castle has been the ancestral home of the Percys, the Earls and Dukes of Northumberland. The title Duke of Northumberland was held by Hugh Smithson, father of James Smithson, whose bequest to the United States founded the Smithsonian Institution "for the increase and diffusion of knowledge."

'DOUBLE DELIGHT,' a large-flowered, fragrant hybrid tea developed in 1986, offers a lesson in the art of rose breeding. In the Folger Rose Garden, it grows between its parents, the bright rose-colored seed parent 'Granada' and the pale pink pollen parent 'Garden Party.' Their offspring 'Double Delight' inherited from 'Garden Party' a pale pink center and from 'Granada' a bright rose color in the surrounding ruff of petals. Like 'Granada,' 'Double Delight' is quite fragrant.

'KNOCKOUT' is a cherry red shrub rose with amazing disease resistance introduced in 2000. William Radler, who bred 'Knockout,' ground up and then applied infected leaves to the rose bushes he developed. To further guarantee the spread of disease, he used overhead watering. By fall, it was easy to see which plants were diseased and which were resistant. 'Knockout' stood out as highly resistant to disease.

Like the roses, the Gur-Karma-Rana Fountain in the garden has a story to tell. A nineteenth-century antique, the three-tiered, cast-iron fountain was manufactured by the J. W. Fiske Iron Works Company of New York in the mid-1880s. Ravaged by time, the fountain, which once stood in the Quadrangle, fell into disrepair. A generous contribution by Narinder and Rajinder K. Keith paid for its restoration. In a tribute to the Keith family, the fountain's name is made up of the first few letters of several family members' first names. Placed around the fountain, the better to enjoy its cooling mist on a hot summer day, are Victorian-style benches and flower-filled urns, several of which are antiques. The fountain area, convenient to the Mall but comfortably apart from it, is a fine place to sit and enjoy the panoply of roses and their companion plants in the Folger Rose Garden.

On a hot summer day, the Gur-Karma-Rana Fountain sends a cooling mist through the garden. Its unusual name represents the first few letters of the names of members of the Keith family, who sponsored the restoration of this nineteenth-century antique.

Integrated Pest Management

The Kathrine Dulin Folger Rose Garden is maintained using integrated pest management. This system is a way of controlling garden and agricultural pests by combining practices that are the least hazardous to people and the environment. IPM aims to reduce the use of pesticides while keeping pests at an acceptable level.

An important tenet of IPM is determining what an acceptable level is. Imperfection with some insect damage is deemed tolerable. Pests are controlled, not eradicated. Another tenet of IPM is preventive cultivation. The best plant varieties for local conditions are chosen. They are kept healthy by proper care and preventive actions, such as the removal of diseased plants to avoid the spread of disease. Plants are carefully monitored to spot pests before they get out of control. Pests are identified so that information about their reproductive cycles and their development can aid in controlling them.

If insects reach unacceptable levels, control is begun. Used first are simple mechanical means, including trapping or handpicking pests from an affected plant. Biological controls, such as beneficial predators, are the next step. If all else fails, synthetic pesticides are applied sparingly and at the appropriate phases in the pest's life cycle. Horticultural oils and insecticidal soaps are preferred over synthetic pyrethroids (insecticides).

Smithsonian horticulturists keep a close watch on the roses and perennials to address any pest problems that arise. Although some insects are harmful to the plants, ladybird beetles (Coccinellidae) are among the insects that are considered beneficial because they feed on damaging pests.

MARY LIVINGSTON RIPLEY GARDEN

High summer brings a crowd of flowering perennials to the Ripley Garden (opposite). Against the deep green of a towering arborvitae (Thuja occidentalis), daylilies (Hemerocallis 'Mango Thrills'), lilies (Lilium 'Sweetheart'), Helen's flower (Helenium 'Mardi Gras'), blanket flowers (Gaillardia 'Oranges and Lemons'), and variegated honeysuckle (Lonicera 'Baggeson's Gold') add warm notes of orange and gold.

Flanked by mature trees and shrubs, the Mall entrance to this jewel of a garden only hints at the expanse and richness within. Those who venture past this entrance into the Mary Livingston Ripley Garden, tucked between the Arts and Industries Building and the Hirshhorn Museum and Sculpture Garden, find themselves in a surprisingly spacious fountain courtyard. Around the antique acanthus fountain, benches nestle in quiet alcoves and urns brim with foliage and flowers—furnishing a peaceful retreat from the crowds of the nation's capital. Beyond the courtyard, a winding walkway meanders to another entrance on Independence Avenue. In curvilinear beds along the walkway's length, an exuberant grouping of colorful and textural annuals, perennials, and, in summer, bold tropicals intermingle around uncommon shrubs and trees.

Mindful of the Smithsonian's scientific and educational missions, the horticulturist Janet Draper purposefully mixes as many plants as possible to demonstrate the range of ornamental plants that can be grown. Unusual as well as common ornamentals come together in refreshing, original combinations, enabling visitors to observe how these plants grow and which strategies they have evolved for pollination. The result is a plant lover's paradise, home to—at last count—more than one thousand different plants and bulbs. To experience them all, visitors should stroll slowly around the courtyard and along the entire length of this half-acre garden. What is quickly apparent is that this amazing variety and number of plants coexist in remarkable harmony, combining to create the brilliant tableaux for which this garden is renowned.

The Ripley Garden meanders between Independence Avenue and the Mall. Viewed from a quiet alcove, its fountain courtyard features winding brick paths and numerous containers brimming with annuals.

So delightful and successful a garden as this would seem to be the happy result of long-entertained and carefully laid plans. In fact the Mary Livingston Ripley Garden was never included in any of the plans for the Mall's development. The space it occupies might have become a parking lot if it had not been for a series of unrelated but fortuitous events.

The first of these was the construction from 1969 to 1971 of the Ninth Street tunnel, which, along with the Twelfth Street tunnel, forms a spur of the Southwest-Southeast Freeway passing under the Mall. Completed in December 1971, the tunnel's roof formed a level expanse between the Arts and Industries Building and the site now housing the Hirshhorn Museum, a space originally called the Plaza. Until 1976 this plaza was used for the storage of building equipment during renovation of the Arts and Industries Building. Construction of the Hirshhorn Museum in 1974 included a wall along the museum's western boundary. This wall, with the sense of enclosure it brought, was a first step toward the development of a garden.

The future garden received some of its first permanent plantings in 1976. After Smithsonian Secretary S. Dillon Ripley's family home in Litchfield, Connecticut, was destroyed by fire, venerable specimens of winter creeper (Euonymus fortunei 'Sarcoxie') were rescued. Pruned and trained as espaliers for fifty years by Ripley's mother, they found a new home on the west side of the Hirshhorn wall. At the time, the only other inhabitants of the space were eight American elms (Ulmus americana), the street trees specified by the McMillan Plan for the Mall.

Even with the euonymus espaliers and the elms, the future garden remained little more than a pass-through between the Mall and Independence Avenue. Nevertheless Secretary Ripley's wife, Mary Livingston Ripley, who had been inspired by a garden for the blind in San Francisco's Golden Gate Park, envisioned the space as a "sensory garden" for the enjoyment of handicapped and other visitors to the Smithsonian. To develop such a garden, Mary Ripley appealed to the Smithsonian Women's Committee for financial support. The committee responded with generous funding for what was then dubbed the East Garden.

Mary Livingston Ripley, at the center, visits the garden named for her. She is joined by Valerie Burden, representing the Smithsonian Women's Committee, and James R. Buckler, the first director of the Smithsonian's Office of Horticulture.

A dusting of snow lends an enchanting note to the Ripley Garden at night (opposite top).

The garden's brick walkways (opposite bottom) were laid out to encourage visitors to slow down and enjoy the landscape. Raised beds make it possible for people in wheelchairs to get close to plantings such as Euphorbia 'Diamond Frost,' at the left, and coleus (Solenostemon × hybrida), at the right.

In July 1978 the local architecture firm Hugh Newell Jacobsen and Associates was awarded the contract for the design of the East Garden, and work was begun. The Jacobsen plan called for brick paving and beds. Designed to encourage visitors to slow down and enjoy the plants along the way, a sinuous walkway would meander between richly planted beds that echoed and embraced its curves. Nearer the Mall end of the garden, retaining walls would hold planting beds at the proper height for a person in a wheelchair.

During construction, the raised beds posed a problem. The elms along the east side of Ninth Street were growing at ground level. To bring the top of their root balls level with the soil surface in the new raised beds, several had to be lifted. To accomplish this with minimal damage, four elms were dug out by hand and hoisted with a crane before their holes could be backfilled and the walls built around them. It is a tribute to the skill of the arborists that three of the four elms they replanted survived. In all, five of the original eight elms remain. The path and walls were completed in 1981.

A bold tropical, Solanum quitoense—with its enormous green leaves studded with purple thorns—attracts attention in the Ripley Garden. In temperate climates such as Washington's, it is an annual.

In 1988 the garden was renamed by the Smithsonian Women's Committee and dedicated to the woman who had worked so hard to bring it into being, Mary Livingston Ripley. Scholar, enthusiastic gardener, and ardent supporter of the Smithsonian, Mary Ripley was a founding member of the committee and had served as its president. Plaques located at each end of the garden read: "This garden was created by the Smithsonian Institution Women's Committee in honor of their founder and friend." For the support and care of the garden, in 1994 Kathrine Dulin Folger (*see page 56*) of Washington, D.C., and Palm Beach, Florida, established an endowment fund.

Tulips (Tulipa 'Snow Parrot,' 'Zurel,' 'Violet Beauty,' and 'Negrita') in the Ripley Garden (opposite) are paired with an underplanting of Johnny jump-ups (Viola cornuta 'Blackberry Cream' and 'Antique Plum').

Mary Ripley's efforts and influence set into motion the metamorphosis of a space once earmarked for parking into one of Washington's most beloved and inspirational gardens. Today bump-outs in the planting beds indicate places where elms once grew. In their vacated spaces, a pleasing variety of ornamentals have taken up residence—presenting something to captivate the eye in every season.

A Triumph of Nature

To protect the Mary Livingston Ripley Garden from foot traffic during the presidential inauguration of Barack Obama, six-foot fences were installed at both ends of the garden. On the morning of January 20, 2009, crowds began to arrive at 4:30 A.M. Two hours later, the crush to reach the Mall was so great that the barrier closest to Independence Avenue was breached and the throng pushed through.

The crowd flooded through the garden like a break in a levee. The next morning dawned on near-total destruction. Plants were flattened. The evergreens had been trampled. It seemed that the garden was dead. Amazingly, as winter turned into early spring, hellebores that had been turned to dust bloomed and were followed by the emergence of many of the presumed deceased in a triumph of nature over adversity.

During the inauguration of President Barack Obama, crowds anxious to get to the Mall trampled the garden (top and center). Although it seemed as if nothing could survive the stampede, spring brought forth the usual bulbs: guinea hen flowers (Fritillaria meleagris) and grape hyacinths (Muscari armeniacum) (bottom).

In winter the coral bark maple (*Acer palmatum* 'Sango-kaku') shows off improbably bright, coral-colored branches, while two mature Harry Lauder's walking sticks (*Corylus avellana* 'Contorta') function as living sculpture, dangling catkins on wondrously contorted branches. Elsewhere the tiny flowers of evergreen thorny eleagnus (*Elaeagnus pungens*) send sweet scent into the cold winter air. Weeks later a new perfume wafts abroad as two witch hazels (*Hamamelis* 'Arnold Promise') open their fragrant flowers over a carpet of snowdrops (*Galanthus nivalis*) and Lenten roses (*Helleborus* × *hybridus*). Dozens of glory-of-the-snow (*Chionodoxa luciliae*) and squills (*Scilla* sp.) follow, dovetailing with daffodils and tulips.

Spring in the Ripley Garden may be magical, but summer's display puts it over the top. An extravaganza of colors, textures, shapes, and fragrances greets the visitor throughout the warm months, as bold tropicals that have overwintered in Smithsonian Gardens greenhouses consort with flowering annuals, fine-textured grasses, and perennials with intriguing flowers and foliage. It is a public-pleasing display. Visitors who fill out a comment form are asked the question, "What would add to your enjoyment of the garden?" Whether the person answering hails from Bulgaria or Minnesota, India or Capitol Hill, the most frequent response is, "Nothing. It's perfect."

When entering the Ripley Garden from Independence Avenue, visitors are welcomed by an elaborately planted shade garden, beautiful in all seasons. Soloman's seal (Polygonatum odoratum var. pluriflorum 'Variegatum') rises above a bed of foamflower (Tiarella 'Spanish Cross'), flanked by purple toadflax (Linaria purpurea) and columbine (Aquilegia sp.).

Sculpture Garden and Plaza

Hirshhorn Museum and Sculpture Garden

The Hirshhorn Museum boasts two open-air "galleries" where visitors can enjoy sculptures in garden settings: a paved plaza around and underneath the circular museum building as well as a sunken garden located across Jefferson Drive on the Mall. These display areas, which together provide more than four acres dedicated to modern art, were essential components of the museum's initial conception in 1966. In that year the entrepreneur Joseph H. Hirshhorn

President Lyndon B. Johnson and Lady Bird Johnson join Joseph Hirshhorn and his wife, Olga, at the museum's groundbreaking in 1969, five years before it opened.

(1899–1981) agreed to donate more than 5,500 works of art to the Smithsonian; in his will he bequeathed an additional 6,000 works, and the museum has steadily acquired many others.

Although Hirshhorn had collected thousands of paintings, his collection was internationally renowned for its modern sculptures. These ranged from small studies to life-sized figures and monumental abstract constructions. Round Hill, his home in Greenwich, Connecticut, featured dozens of sculptures installed on twenty-two rolling acres of lawn with a view of the Manhattan skyline. It was both his wish and the Smithsonian's intention to place many of them outdoors in Washington, in a prominent location on the Mall.

After Hirshhorn made his generous founding gift of art, obstacles from the financial to the political delayed the design and final approval of the museum and its garden. The museum's architect, Gordon Bunshaft (1909–90) of Skidmore, Owings and Merrill—himself an art collector—was sensitive to the need to devise indoor and outdoor settings that suit sculpture. His proposals also had to dovetail with official plans for the Mall. The new museum's site, a square lot on Independence Avenue, was across the Mall from another square lot on Constitution Avenue where the National Gallery of Art hoped to put a sculpture garden. That plot was already dominated by a large circular pool in the center. Seeking symmetry on the Mall, Bunshaft thus planned the Hirshhorn in the shape of a circle: a massive open cylinder rests on four massive piers, with a circular fountain in the center courtyard.

Aristide Maillol's Nymph (1953) is sheltered by a weeping beech (Fagus sylvatica 'Pendula') (opposite). At the left is a Japanese black pine (Pinus thunbergii).

Aristide Maillol
French, 1861–1944
Nymph (Central Figure for
"The Three Graces")
1938, cast by 1953
Bronze
Gift of Joseph H. Hirshhorn, 1966
66.3335

An open cylinder set on four massive piers, the Hirshhorn Museum occupies the former site of the Army Medical Museum (1886). It was built of a mix of precast concrete and a crushed aggregate of pink granite. The same material was originally used for the surrounding square plaza but has since been replaced with rings of granite as envisioned by the architect Gordon Bunshaft.

The Sculpture Garden

In Bunshaft's original plan, the museum building was to overlook a large rectangular garden extending across the Mall to abut the National Gallery's lot. To avoid interrupting the Mall's open vista, Bunshaft designed this garden to rest in a sunken area, surrounded by low walls. The garden would consist primarily of a large reflecting pool echoing at a right angle the larger reflecting pool fronting the Lincoln Memorial at the Mall's west end; sculptures were to be displayed around the pool's periphery.

When critics insisted that the Mall be kept open between the Capitol and the Washington Monument, this design was abandoned. Benjamin Forgey, architecture critic of the *Washington Star*, suggested a solution that was adopted: the rectangular sunken garden was reduced drastically in size and rotated ninety degrees to lie alongside Jefferson Drive across from the Hirshhorn Museum. To make room for the sculptures, the reflecting pool became only a small element in the center. Bunshaft was inspired by the radical simplification of minimalist art and especially by the open spaces of Japanese dry gardens and Zen rock gardens. When the museum opened in October 1974, its two-level, 1.3-acre sculpture garden was as strikingly spare as the doughnut-shaped building itself.

Bunshaft designed a sunken sculpture garden with a wonderful sense of intimacy away from the hubbub on the Mall. However, the minimalist design and materials, combined with a lack of greenery, resulted in a space that retained heat in Washington's torrid summers, making visits then uncomfortable.

After Lester Collins was commissioned to renovate and redesign the Sculpture Garden in 1979, ramps were installed on the Mall side to make it more universally accessible; several discrete display areas and trees were also added (above). Sugar maple (Acer saccharum), crape myrtle (Lagerstroemia indica 'Natchez'), and Japanese black pine (Pinus thunbergii) now surround a verdant lawn. Luxuriant plantings and lawn (right) make the garden infinitely more comfortable.

Boston ivy (Parthenocissus tricuspidata) and climbing hydrangea (Hydrangea anomala ssp. petiolaris) frame Judith Shea's Post Balzac (1991).

The central area was placed more than eighteen feet below street level, effectively blocking out much of the urban traffic noise and creating a wonderful sense of intimacy and calm in the spirit of Zen meditative spaces. A lone weeping willow stood by the small pool, surrounded by flat areas covered in pale buff pebbles. Aggregate walls of the same pebbles augmented the neutral monochromatic setting, designed to highlight the bronze, metal, and stone sculptures. The anguished figures of Auguste Rodin's *Burghers of Calais* (cast 1953–59) dominated the scene, attracting people at street level to come down and look more closely. Arnoldo Pomodoro's gleaming, golden bronze *Sphere No. 6* (1963–65) appeared to hover in a vast cosmic space. Alexander Calder's kinetic sculpture *Six Dots over a Mountain* (1956) added a splash of red, white, and blue.

Henry Moore's Draped Reclining Figure (1952–53) is set off by a Japanese black pine (Pinus thunbergii).

In Washington's torrid summers, the stone and concrete of the garden, which stands open to the southern sun, retained heat and was passed over by breezes, so the outdoor room became oppressively hot. And with the passage of the Americans with Disabilities Act, the Smithsonian was required to install accessibility ramps from the Mall level. In 1979, therefore, the Hirshhorn Museum decided to close the garden for a major renovation.

The noted landscape architect Lester Collins (1914–93) was commissioned to redesign the space. In addition to installing a symmetrical pair of long ramps on the Mall side, he replaced the pebbled areas with paved paths around trees, shrubs, and lawn, transforming the space into a lush garden. At the request of the Hirshhorn's director and curator, Abram Lerner, Collins used plants to subdivide the garden into discrete display areas. To support the plantings, a subterranean water supply was expanded. When the garden reopened in 1981, the new plantings provided a more welcoming and comfortable place for visitors.

To cover most of the aggregate walls that remained from Bunshaft's design, Collins strategically used climbing hydrangea (Hydrangea anomala ssp. petiolaris), which are trimmed to provide a halo effect around certain sculptures. Because Aristide Maillol's Nymph (1953) had previously suffered some damage to her back, she is now protected in her new location, sheltered by two weeping beeches (Fagus sylvatica 'Pendula'). As the sun traverses from east to west, the Japanese black pine trees (Pinus thunbergii) provide a changing pattern of shadows on the sculptures, such as Henry Moore's Seated Woman (1957–58).

Also at the request of Lerner, Collins's design incorporated several features to improve protection of certain sculptures that had been unintentionally harmed by some of the 700,000 annual visitors who could not refrain from touching the most popular works of art. Of greatest concern was Rodin's Burghers of Calais, often a climbing target for visitors seeking photo opportunities. Collins's new design featured a raised square of grass fringed by granite at the garden's east end to separate this masterpiece from the other displays. On the west side, Joan Miró's fantastical Lunar Bird (1966–67) stands on an identical raised square; when visitors continued to climb on it, Smithsonian Gardens staff planted a protective bed of fine-textured Mexican feather grass (Nassella tenuissima), which is a delicate green in summer and buff colored in winter. In addition to protecting the sculpture, the fine-textured grass presents a pleasing contrast to the sculpture's massiveness. Similarly, because Pomodoro's Sphere No. 6 is too easily scratched by human touch, it stands apart in a square bed of texturally contrasting lily turf (Liriope muscari).

To discourage climbing, Joan Miró's Lunar Bird (1966–67) was installed on a raised platform surrounded by a bed of Mexican feather grass (Nasella tenuissima). As well as protecting the sculpture, the fine-textured grass is an excellent contrast with the sculpture's smooth curves.

Yoko Ono's Wish Tree for Washington

During the Cherry Blossom Festival in 2007, the artist Yoko Ono presented the Hirshhorn Museum and Sculpture Garden with a Japanese dogwood (*Cornus kousa*) on which visitors to the garden could hang wishes. It was one of ten trees exhibited around Washington during the festival as part of her ongoing Wish Tree project. After the installation, the wishes on the Washington trees were collected and became part of Ono's *Imagine Peace Tower* in Reykjavik, Iceland.

The practice of tying wishes to trees is one that Ono remembers from her childhood in Japan. In Shinto temple gardens there, people can buy paper fortunes (*omikuji*) and wooden plaques (*ema*) on which to write wishes. These are then hung on trees or special stands. If a wish tree is very large, such as the one at Tokyo's Shinto Meiji Shrine, people place their wishes around its trunk.

Of the ten wish trees showcased in the nation's capital by Yoko Ono, only the one in the Hirshhorn Sculpture Garden remains as a permanent installation. It is currently available for wishing from Memorial Day through Labor Day.

The Plaza

Three southern magnolias (Magnolia grandiflora) were growing on the Hirshhorn site before the museum was built. They were protected during construction and now serve as an evergreen background for Lucio Fontana's Spatial Concept: Nature (1963).

When the Hirshhorn Museum and its 2.7-acre plaza were built in 1969–74, cost overruns prevented the Smithsonian from implementing Gordon Bunshaft's original plans for materials. Instead of cladding the building in pale pink granite and the plaza surface in dark granite, buff-colored aggregate (as used in the original garden) was substituted. After this inexpensive material degraded, the Hirshhorn invited the landscape architect and tree expert James Urban of Annapolis, Maryland, to renovate the entire plaza in 1993. Deteriorating surfaces were replaced with the paving pattern of concentric rings of dark and pale granite originally stipulated in Bunshaft's plan. In the northeast corner a new ramp and gate allowed access to the adjacent Mary Livingston Ripley Garden.

In the new design, four aerial hedges of neatly trimmed flowering crabapple trees (*Malus* sp.) divide the plaza garden into six separate rooms for displaying sculptures. The floor of each room is neatly trimmed lawn that curves along its innermost edge to echo the building's cylindrical shape. The outer edge follows the straight walls that enclose the entire square plaza. In one sylvan room, Juan Muñoz's *Last Conversation Piece* (1995), a group of five life-sized bronze figures, balances on punching-bag bases. In another, Tony Cragg's giant image of old rubber stamps, *Subcommittee* (1991), mocks the tool of bureaucracy. The five components of Lucio Fontana's *Spatial Concept: Nature* (1963) are sited on an expanse of lawn backed by three enormous southern magnolias (*Magnolia grandiflora*). These magnolias were growing on the site before the Hirshhorn Museum was built and were protected through the initial years of construction and the subsequent renovations. Their massive size and the bold texture of their evergreen foliage form a splendid backdrop to the sculptures.

A pleasing affinity between sculpture and garden is evident in the Hirshhorn plaza and the sculpture garden. Sculptures add powerful focal points that lend excitement and mystery to the garden; the lawn and plantings create dramatic settings that enhance and protect the sculptures. In natural surroundings, visitors can enjoy both in the changing light of day and during all seasons of the year.

The Hirshhorn's sinuous edges echo the supple forms of many of the sculptures in the nearby garden. A splashing fountain at the heart of the plaza welcomes visitors to the museum.

Around the plaza's paved area, spacious expanses of lawn—divided by hedges of neatly trimmed flowering crabapple trees (Malus sp.)—serve as individual outdoor display areas for large and multicomponent works such as Juan Muñoz's Last Conversation Piece (1995).

WALLED TERRACES

NATIONAL AIR AND SPACE MUSEUM

Walled terraces step up from the street level to lessen the impact of the immense National Air and Space Museum (opposite). Originally planted in lawn and shrubs, the terraces were redesigned in 1996 with trees, shrubs, and swaths of tough, easy-care perennials such as catnip (Nepeta cataria).

When Congress appropriated funds for the construction of the National Air and Space Museum in 1971, the architect Gyo Obata of Hellmuth, Obata and Kassabaum was charged with a daunting task. He was asked to design a building commodious enough to house the world's largest collection of historic aircraft and spacecraft. From kites to gliders to airplanes and rockets, little that had to do with flight was small enough to fit into standard display cases. Yet the building also had to avoid overpowering the nearby Capitol.

The Smithsonian collection of flight-related exhibits had been accumulating since the close of the Centennial Exhibition in Philadelphia in 1876, when a group of kites was acquired from the Chinese Imperial Commission. As it grew, the collection gained a name, the National Aircraft Collection, and beginning in 1919 filled a Quonset hut that had been erected in the Castle's South Yard in 1917. Planes such as Charles Lindbergh's *Spirit of St. Louis*, presented to the Smithsonian in 1928, were hung from the rafters of the Arts and Industries Building. Because they were too large to be housed there, rockets donated to the National Air Museum, established in 1946, were eventually lined up along the building's side, creating what was called Rocket Row. The space race of the 1950s and 1960s did more than change the name of the proposed museum from the National Air Museum to the National Air and Space Museum; it also produced monumental paraphernalia from space travel.

The museum is large enough to accommodate huge exhibits associated with flight but discreet enough not to overwhelm nearby buildings. Along with the terraces, steel and glass atria break up the building's mass, visually diminishing its size.

Ad Astra ("to the stars"), a 1976
commission by the American
sculptor Richard Lippold, rises in
front of the north entrance
of the museum.

When the new National Air and Space Museum opened on July 1, 1976, in time
for the American Bicentennial, it was clear that Obata's design had succeeded in
accommodating behemoth exhibits without overwhelming the Capitol.
Composed of a string of cubes that align with recesses of the National Gallery of
Art's West Building across the Mall, the building is faced with the same pink
Tennessee marble. Its cubes are connected by steel and glass atria where large
exhibits of airplanes, missiles, and spacecraft can be viewed from the inside
against the sky. From the outside, the glass walls have the effect of lightening
the museum, a 636,000-square-foot mass that takes up two city blocks.

Another factor in diminishing the bulk of this immense structure is that it is
tethered to the ground by seven acres of terraces. More than two acres are
actually roof-top planters. In 1975 the terraces were planted in plains of lawn and
shrubs. The plantings were redesigned in 1996 by the Smithsonian Gardens
landscape architects Paul Lindell and Karen Swanson, who added numerous
trees that are gracefully accommodated on the large terraces. Among them are a
group of Forest Pansy redbuds (*Cercis canadensis* 'Forest Pansy') with glowing
garnet foliage, forests of river birch (*Betula nigra*), and a legion of crape myrtles
(*Lagerstroemia* × *hybrida*). The trees compose a softening fringe against the
museum's great walls, aiding in obscuring the line between the ground plane
and the building and thus visually lessening the museum's mass.

The massive size and length of the National Air and Space Museum and its east-west orientation actually divide the garden into two microclimates. The south side basks in the sun and is always several degrees warmer than the north side. The sun-baked south terrace is warm enough to support dwarf palmettos (*Sabal minor*) and hardy bananas (*Musa basjoo*). Depending on the season, the shady north side either benefits or suffers from wind funneled down the Mall. Both sides can be challenging to plants, especially those growing in containers.

In 1996, when the planters over the museum's garage were re-waterproofed, Lindell and Swanson replaced swards of thirsty lawn on the terraces with perennials. The plants they chose were tough enough to survive in planters during Washington's sultry summers and windy winters and look good while doing so. They require far less maintenance than turf grass. In sunny places, great carpets of flowering perennials include catmint (*Nepeta* sp.), daylilies (*Hemerocallis* sp.), coneflowers (*Echinacea purpurea*), and black-eyed Susans (*Rudbeckia hirta*). Herbaceous plants alternate with shrubs, dwarf fothergilla (*Fothergilla gardenii*), shrubby cinquefoil (*Potentilla fruticosa*), and summersweet (*Clethra alnifolia*).

Ground cover flourishes in the shade of trees. Lily turf (*Liriope muscari*), garnet-colored coral bells (*Heuchera* sp.), and flowing yellow hakone grass (*Hakonechloa macra* 'Aureola') blanket the ground with color. Hostas (*Hosta* sp.) and apple green palm sedge (*Carex muskingumensis*) are super-sturdy perennials that dovetail with spring flowering bulbs and camouflage their after-bloom foliage.

Next to the building, a chaste tree (Vitex agnus-castus) blooms lavender in the summer. Later on, its dense green crown casts cooling shade.

Dozens of trees growing in the walled terraces soften the building's crisp edges and obscure the line between the ground plane and the building.

85

The richly varied plant collection turns the museum terraces into a garden that is handsome in all seasons. There is always something to intrigue the eye:

In WINTER the leafless trunks and branches of the garden's trees present living sculpture. Saucer magnolias (*Magnolia × soulangeana*) expose silvery, muscular limbs that wrinkle at their junctures. Native river birches (*Betula nigra*) exfoliate their bark in craggy fissures. When crape myrtles lose their bark, they become smoother, sleeker, and tinted with pale copper.

SPRING is an explosion of bloom. It begins with the precocious flowers of Japanese apricot (*Prunus mume*) and Lenten roses (*Helleborus × hybridus*) and is followed by legions of bulbs: daffodils (*Narcissus sp.*) and Siberian squills (*Scilla siberica*) under star magnolias (*Magnolia stellata*) and weeping cherries (*Prunus subhirtella var. pendula*). Spectacular yellow woods (*Cladrastis kentukea*) at the north-western end of the garden dangle white wisteria-like flowers that scent the air.

Flowers bloom in the walled terraces from earliest spring until frost. From left to right are pansies (Viola 'Ultima Morpho'), spirea (Spirea japonica 'Shiro-bana'), verbena shrub (Lantana 'New Citrus Blend'), and black-eyed Susans (Rudbeckia sp.).

SUMMER is lush. Swaths of perennials—Siberian iris (*Iris sibirica*), Stokes' aster (*Stokesia laevis*), and catmint (*Nepeta × faassenii*)—mingle with flowering shrubs, such as shrubby cinquefoil (*Dasiphora floribunda*), chaste trees (*Vitex agnus-castus*), and Japanese spirea (*Spiraea japonica*). Purple smoke trees (*Cotinus coggygria*) bear airy panicles of tiny flowers that look like puffs of pink smoke.

FALL is dazzling. Prairie dropseed (*Sporobolus heterolepis*), a native grass, glistens in the September sunshine and wafts its singular cilantro-like fragrance abroad, while another native grass, river oats (*Chasmanthium latifolium*), dangles pretty seed heads on gracefully arched stems. The brilliant red foliage of chokeberry (*Photinia pyrifolia*) and Virginia sweetspire (*Itea virginica*) contrasts with the banana yellow autumn color of bottlebrush buckeyes (*Aesculus parviflora*) and yellow woods (*Cladrastis kentukea*).

Shade lovers such as these hostas (Hosta 'Hyacinthina' and 'Sun Power') grow lush under the leafy cover of trees. Because the National Air and Space Museum is so large, different plantings thrive in microclimates on its south and north sides.

A great place from which to take it all in is the glass-paneled restaurant at the museum's eastern end. Even better on a fine day is a leisurely stroll around the museum on the inner terrace next to the building. Located away from the mobbed entrances, the inner terrace is richly planted and delightfully uncrowded. At the western end of the museum is a paved area for moving large exhibits in and out of the building through a great door in the west wall. At other times it becomes a pedestrian walkway where it is possible to admire Alejandro Otero's sculpture *Delta Solar* (1977), eat lunch, or simply relax in the shade.

On the eastern end of the National Air and Space Museum, daylilies (Hemerocallis 'Stella d'Oro') cover a bank that steps down from the museum's glass-walled restaurant.

Sculptures Celebrating Flight

Slipping the "surly bonds of earth" demands profound knowledge of scientific principles and the earth's atmosphere. Three sculptures on the grounds of the National Air and Space Museum celebrate the triumph of flight and address its practical considerations:

Wind moves the stainless-steel panels of *Delta Solar* (1977). This kinetic sculpture, located on the museum's western end, is the work of Alejandro Otero (1921–90), a Venezuelan artist and writer who lived for periods in New York, Washington, and Paris. In the 1960s he began to create large-scale public art he called civic sculptures. *Delta Solar* is a gift from the people of Venezuela.

Continuum (1976), near the museum's south entrance, is an artistic expression of the scientific principles and ideas explored inside. Its architect-sculptor, Charles O. Perry, explains that it is "an exploration of the Möbius strip, a product of pure mathematics formed by joining two ends of a strip of paper after giving one end a 180-degree twist, thus creating one edge."

Paying homage to the human quest to explore the universe, the sculpture *Ad Astra* (Latin for "to the stars") is located at the museum's Mall entrance (*see page 84*). It rises 115 feet and is topped with a constellation of wire stars. *Ad Astra* was created for the museum in 1976 by the American sculptor Richard Lippold (1915–2002), a former industrial designer noted for geometric works that use wire.

Delta Solar (1977), a kinetic sculpture by the Venezuelan artist Alejandro Otero, moves with the wind. It is situated at the western end of the National Air and Space Museum, near a welcoming pedestrian mall.

NATIVE LANDSCAPE

NATIONAL MUSEUM OF THE AMERICAN INDIAN

On the grounds of the National Museum of the American Indian, columbine (Aquilegia canadensis), a dainty woodland wildflower, grows beside the sturdy, exfoliating trunk of an American sycamore (Platanus occidentalis).

A spiral lunar pattern at the museum's south entrance (opposite) recalls a petroglyph of the nineteen-year cycle between lunar standstills. In the background is a cherished native tree, an American elm (Ulmus americana).

Occupying one of the National Mall's last available sites, the National Museum of the American Indian opened on September 21, 2004. From its conception, this museum was meant to be unique among the museums on the Mall. Its express purpose was not merely to exhibit artifacts from the past, but additionally to reflect living indigenous cultures of the Americas and to present these distinct perspectives to the nation and the world.

Native peoples were involved in every aspect of the museum's development. Artists, elders, and leaders from nearly 150 native communities from the Arctic to the Galapagos were consulted. Their ideas were collected in a planning document entitled "The Way of the People." In this compilation, indigenous peoples from diverse communities in different parts of the Western Hemisphere came together and affirmed a holistic world view in which all things—people and animals, plants and planets, rocks, rivers, and land—are alive, connected, and interdependent. Kevin Gover (Pawnee), second director of the museum, notes that there is "an ancient and deeply held Indian concept that the earth herself is a living, sentient being."

Douglas Cardinal (Blackfoot), an architect from Ottawa, Canada, designed a building for the museum that strongly contrasts with the more linear architecture around it on the Mall. Clad in Kasota stone, a 350-million-year-old limestone from Minnesota, the undulating structure suggests a rock formation with lines as fluid as those of a mesa honed by wind and water. The design team members—the architect Johnpaul Jones (Cherokee/Choctaw), ethnobotanist Donna House (Navajo/Oneida), and artist Ramona Sakiestewa (Hopi)—helped develop and implement Cardinal's vision, carefully considering the significance of the plantings and the exterior design elements. Building and landscape form an integrated whole.

Mindful of its position in the universe, the museum's main entrance faces east to greet the morning sun. At this entrance, a vast circular pattern in the paving stones displays the position of planets visible on November 28, 1989, the day legislation was enacted to create the museum. A spiral lunar pattern marks the museum's south entrance—it recalls a spiral petroglyph atop Chaco Canyon's Fajada Butte that marks the nineteen-year cycle between lunar standstills.

CARDINAL DIRECTION MARKERS

As well as indicating the cardinal directions, the four stone markers represent different epochs in the earth's history. The southern marker is a rock of the Cretaceous period, moved to Washington from the ancestral lands of the Yagán people near Tierra del Fuego, Chile.

The four rocks that serve as direction markers tie the museum to the site, creating balance at their confluence. Each comes from a different geological epoch, representing stages in Earth's life, and was carefully transported and sited in its original orientation. The native communities that selected and donated these rocks received in symbolic exchange pieces of the same Kasota limestone used to construct the museum.

The north marker, from the Tlicho (Dligo) community north of Yellowknife in Canada's Northwest Territories, is Acasta gneiss from the Basins Group era of the Hadean eon. At about four billion years old, it is likely the oldest known exposed rock in the world.

The east marker, a 544-million-year-old quartzite stone from the Cambrian period, is from Maryland's Monocacy Valley. The 5,000-pound stone was positioned to face the Capitol in hopes of maintaining a positive relationship between native peoples and the federal government.

The south marker, an ambassador from the Yagán people of Isla Navarino in Chile, dates from the Cretaceous period and is between 65 and 145 million years old.

The west marker, the youngest stone, came from the Keamoku lava flow (ca. 1662) at Hawai'i Volcanoes National Park on the island of Hawaii. Because Hawaiians consider stones to be living beings, this one, named Kane Po, will return to Hawaii after twenty years. Another stone will then take its place.

Like the building, the landscape—which surrounds the museum and takes up almost three quarters of the site—displays a full awareness of its geographical orientation. On its boundaries, four great stone markers indicate the cardinal directions. Huge boulders known as Grandfather Rocks are the landscape's elders: retaining memories of ancestors, protecting the site, and representing the longevity of native peoples and their relationship to the land. An outdoor theater, a fire pit for ceremonies and cooking, and an offering area, sheltered for privacy by great boulders, allow programs to be held outdoors.

Selected from a quarry in Alma, Quebec, the Grandfather Rocks retain memories of ancestors, protect the site, and represent the longevity of native peoples. They were blessed in Canada by the Montagnais First Nations people and in Washington by a member of Virginia's Monacan Nation.

A primary goal of the design was to honor the native nations of the Washington, D.C., region (the project's hosts) by reintroducing the area's indigenous landscape on this site. The aim was to establish the history and the distinct character of the site as it existed before the Europeans' arrival. To acquire a sense of the natural landscape and its flora, Donna House canoed tributaries of the nearby Potomac River. She then collaborated with landscape architects at EDAW, Inc., and Smithsonian Gardens horticulturists and landscape architects to create a design that both looks natural and sets in motion processes that will make it become natural.

In bold contrast to traditional gardens in which plants are clipped, hedged, and set out in rows, this garden is a spontaneous landscape in which indigenous trees, shrubs, and perennials grow in the community groups and conditions they inhabit in the wild. The first museum exhibit a visitor encounters, it represents an acceptance of nature rather than an effort to control it. The museum's garden is divided into four habitats of the regional landscape as they existed four hundred years ago: forest, wetland, meadow, and cropland. Plants growing in these habitats are neither exotics nor improved hybrids. All are indigenous to the Mid-Atlantic region and were put to use as food, medicine, fiber, or dye or harvested for ceremonial purposes. Each plant in this landscape has an ethnobotanical use for Native American peoples.

THE UPLAND HARDWOOD FOREST

Running along the northern edge of the landscape, adjacent to Jefferson Drive, the upland hardwood forest is the largest habitat, measuring about 24,000 square feet. It reconstitutes woodland that once covered much of the local area and now exists only in remnants such as Rock Creek Park, Washington's urban park. The forest is divided into three zones characterized by varying soil textures and amounts of moisture:

The XERIC ZONE has dry soil that supports plants such as the chinkapin (*Castanea pumila*), Virginia pine (*Pinus virginiana*), and smooth penstemon (*Penstemon digitalis*).

The MESIC ZONE has soil that is moderately moist and supports flowering dogwood (*Cornus florida*) and southern magnolia (*Magnolia grandiflora*).

In the HYDRIC ZONE, where moisture is abundant, species such as water tupelo (*Nyssa aquatica*), American holly (*Ilex opaca*), serviceberry (*Amelanchier arborea*), and red maple (*Acer rubrum*) flourish.

Spring brings not flamboyant rows of tulips but carpets of pristine white bloodroot (*Sanguinaria canadensis*), sky blue Virginia bluebells (*Mertensia virginica*), and the shy flowers of wild ginger (*Asarum canadense*). Instead of brilliantly colored azaleas, spicebush (*Lindera benzoin*) blooms in airy yellow clouds, and mountain laurel (*Kalmia latifolia*) opens delicate flowers of a soft pale pink. Half wild, these plants offer the subtle beauty of a country walk in the midst of the marble capital.

Wild strawberry (Fragaria virginiana) sends out runners that make it an edible groundcover. This species is one of the parents of today's cultivated strawberry.

Peeking out from a ground cover of violet foliage (Viola sp.) are white shooting stars (Dodecatheon meadia) (opposite). In the background is a mass of goldenrod (Solidago sp.) that does not bloom until late summer.

Yellow wakerobin (Trillium luteum) is one of the native ephemerals that bloom in the garden's upland hardwood forest area. It was used medicinally by indigenous peoples to treat a variety of ailments.

Water features distinguish the garden's wetland section. Commemorating the historic Tiber Creek, a waterfall plunges into a stream (right). At the garden's eastern end (opposite), the wetland hosts moisture-loving plants—cattails (Typha sp.), waterlilies (Nymphaea sp.), and manna grass (Glyceria striata)—that are as useful as they are beautiful.

THE WETLAND

On the landscape's eastern end, the hydric zone of the forest meets wetland. Before planning the museum, the design team consulted old maps to learn the site's history. It had once been a swamp, with Tiber Creek, a tidal creek, running through a portion of the site (the creek still exists in an enclosed tunnel beneath the Mall). In a tribute to the erstwhile swampland and creek, the garden includes a 6,000-square-foot wetland and a water feature that tumbles into a "river" along the building's north side.

Today the splash and murmur of water mask traffic sounds. The wetland is serene and especially spectacular in summer, when it is lush with aquatic plants as beautiful as they are useful. The legions of white water lilies (Nymphaea sp.) that float languidly on the pond's surface have roots and leaves that were used as medicine. Elsewhere food plants—wild rice (Zizania aquatica) and cattails (Typha sp.)—rise above the surface of the water along with the craggy trunks of swamp cypress (Taxodium distichum). Buttonbush (Cephalanthus occidentalis), named for fragrant, greenish white balls of flowers, thrives in the rich, moist soil at the water's edge.

THE MEADOW

The meadow on the southwestern side of the museum is bright with wildflowers such as these brown-eyed Susans (Rudbeckia triloba).

On the museum's southwestern side, the landscape is a sunny eastern meadow. In summer black-eyed Susans (Rudbeckia sp.), coneflowers (Echinacea sp.), and goldenrod (Solidago sp.) bloom among grasses (Panicum sp., Andropogon sp.). Fall brings the brilliant red of smooth sumac (Rhus glabra) and slowly turns the grasses to shades of orange and gold. Many of the meadow plants were also used for medicinal purposes.

THE CROPLAND

It is estimated that more than 60 percent of the world's food was first cultivated by the indigenous peoples of the Americas. Tomatoes, corn, beans, squash, and potatoes are just a few of the many foods they cultivated. Traditional Native American crops grow in the cropland habitat on the building's south side. Tobacco is also planted here annually for ceremonial uses. The cropland is planted in three rotations:

SPRING greens are the first food plants to be harvested after the winter. They include the new shoots of such wild plants as dandelions, milkweed, pokeweed, mustard, dock, and watercress.

SUMMER follows with the "three sisters," the classic combination of beans, corn, and squash. Tall corn stalks lend support to bean vines, which fix nitrogen in the soil to nourish the corn and the squash plants, whose big leaves shade the soil to preserve moisture and control weeds. To hold water and slow down its percolation, waffle gardens—composed of multiple squares with raised sides to hold water— are usually planted with tomatoes and peppers as well as with winter crops.

FALL plantings, like those of spring, produce cold-hardy greens, including spinach and mustard greens. These are given to the museum's Mitsitam Cafe, where the chef uses them as the vegetable of the day. Cover crops, such as winter wheat, rye, and barley, are rototilled back into the soil to improve tilth and fertility.

Each year a portion of the traditional cropland area at the National Museum of the American Indian is planted with tobacco (Nicotiana tabacum). Once harvested, some of the leaves are dried and later used by the museum for ceremonial purposes and blessings.

The "three sisters"—a traditional term for the symbiotic relationship among corn, beans, and squash—can also be seen in the cropland (opposite). A corn stalk supports a winding bean vine, while at the stalk's base a squash vine shades the ground to conserve moisture and discourage weeds. Varieties grown here are of Native American origin.

NATIVE PLANTS AND ORGANIC GARDENING

Indigenous plants restore missing pieces of the environment. Not only do they grow well in existing conditions, they also support wildlife by playing roles in the life cycles of the creatures with which they have evolved. For example, spice-bush (*Lindera benzoin*) and swamp milkweed (*Asclepius incarnata*) are the larval host plants for, respectively, eastern tiger swallowtail (*Papilio glaucus*) and monarch (*Danaus plexippus*) butterflies. The scarlet tubular flowers of the cardinal flower (*Lobelia cardinalis*) provide nectar for hummingbirds. The grasses, sunflowers, and coneflowers in the meadow produce seeds that feed birds. Shrubs such as buttonbush, partially submerged in shallow water, shelter inver-tebrates that in turn become food for fish, reptiles, amphibians, and ducks.

The museum's landscape is managed organically. Instead of chemical fertilizer, compost tea nourishes the plants. Integrated pest management practices such as ladybug releases reduce undesirable insect populations. The wetland is kept in balance by beneficial bacteria that break down organic waste. In the cropland, horticulturists use crop rotations as a way to rebuild the soil, tilling vegetation back into the earth to add nutrients.

Buttonbush (Cephalanthus occidentalis), a wetland shrub with spherical flowers, is an important nectar source for the viceroy butterfly (Limenitis archippus).

What began as a reconstruction of a native landscape has now taken on a life of its own. Useful to humans and animals, the ancient plant inhabitants of the region are helping the land revert to its original state. A traditional Native American approach to nature has produced the ultimate eco-friendly garden, something that has special resonance today.

Always Becoming

The artist and filmmaker Nora Naranjo-Morse (Santa Clara Pueblo) created the *Always Becoming* sculpture *in situ* during the summer of 2007. The work consists of five figures: Father, Mother, Little One, Moon Woman, and Mountain Bird. Composed of all natural materials—including black locust branches, clay, straw, sand, and yam vines—the figures were designed to be ephemeral, always becoming something new. Since the sculptures were installed, Little One and Mother have lost some of their smooth clay-plaster coating, revealing the texture of the mud and straw inner layer.

As designed by the artist Nora Naranjo-Morse, the figures in Always Becoming (2007) are in a state of constant flux as the elements—wind, rain, snow—work on their natural materials. From the left are Father, Mother, and Little One.

Butterfly Habitat Garden

A spectacular party marked the opening of the Butterfly Habitat Garden at the National Museum of Natural History on June 4, 1995. Seventy-five young Smithsonian Associates released butterflies into the new garden. As American painted ladies (*Vanessa virginiensis*) fluttered overhead, visitors, museum staff members, and Smithsonian Gardens associates looked on, joined by Eric Carle, author of *The Hungry Caterpillar*.

The concept of the Butterfly Garden was a timely idea that occurred almost simultaneously to staff in two Smithsonian divisions. National Museum of Natural History butterfly specialists Don Harvey and Liz Klafter, who gardened to attract butterflies at their own homes, thought of a butterfly garden as a way to create an outdoor educational experience relating to the museum's mission. When they approached Smithsonian Gardens with the idea, they learned that this division had been considering a similar project.

During the larval stage of a monarch butterfly (Danaus plexippus), a caterpillar feeds on the leaf of common milkweed (Asclepias syriaca).

The two staffs collaborated on a design that converted an existing narrow display garden along the eastern edge of the Natural History Museum's almost five-acre site into a butterfly garden. The goal was to develop a garden that emphasized native plants within four habitats—wetland, meadow, woodland edge, and back yard—and the butterflies and bees that frequent them. Each section was designed to feature fascinating connections between insects and plants, highlight butterfly and bee behavior, and provide basic pollination biology. With the help of a generous grant from the Smithsonian Women's Committee, the Butterfly Habitat Garden came into existence.

The entrance to the Butterfly Habitat Garden (opposite) leads into a smorgasbord of trees, shrubs, and forbs (herbaceous flowering plants) that support butterflies in all stages of their life cycle. Overhead a pawpaw (Asimina triloba) shades a bed of heart-leaved asters (Aster cordifolius). Cardinal flower (Lobelia cardinalis) blooms red in the middle ground.

Five years after its opening, a sizable millennium gift from the Garden Club of America in 2000 allowed the garden to triple in size and provided for installation of granite curbs, walks, and an irrigation system. It also funded the addition of a horseshoe-shaped amphitheater where garden staff and museum educators present programs about butterflies, plants, and related topics to visitors and school groups; this area also serves as a pleasant place to sit and enjoy the surroundings. The design and development by landscape architects with Smithsonian Gardens and entomologists and exhibition staff of the National Museum of Natural History essentially transformed a bleak, concrete-dominated pedestrian causeway along the east side of the Ninth Street tunnel, turning it into a garden habitat and a beautiful urban respite 400 feet long by 40 feet wide.

The best time to visit the Butterfly Habitat Garden is in mid- to late summer, when the perennial nectar plants are in full bloom. Some butterflies that spend winter inside a chrysalis, such as eastern tiger swallowtails (Papilio glaucus), are around as soon as the weather warms up. Others that require warm temperatures, such as monarchs (Danaus plexippus), spend the winter in warm places and return in summer. The peak summer season coincides with the arrival of migrating monarchs making the trip from Mexico.

Butterflies that have been seen in the garden include the American lady (Vanessa cardui), cabbage white (Pieris rapae), eastern comma (Polygonia comma), eastern-tailed blue (Everes comyntas), fiery skipper (Hylephila phyleus), great spangled fritillary (Speyeria cybele), monarch (Danaus plexippus), orange sulphur (Colias eurytheme), question mark (Polygonia interrogationis), red admiral (Vanessa atalanta), red spotted purple (Basilarchia astyanax), silver spotted skipper (Epargyreus clarus), spicebush swallowtail (Pterourus troilus), and variegated skipper (Euptoieta claudia).

The garden is divided into five eighty-foot sections demarcated by groupings of American holly (Ilex opaca). The sections contain some two hundred trees and shrubs and more than two thousand herbaceous plants, all of them known to meet the life-cycle needs of butterflies. Some are host plants, those on which eggs are laid or that are eaten by butterfly larvae. Others provide shelter, while still others are nectar plants whose flowers provide a nutrient source for adult butterflies.

THE BUTTERFLY LIFE CYCLE

A butterfly begins life as an egg, laid on or near a host plant that caterpillars need in order to grow. A tiny wormlike caterpillar (larva) emerges from the egg, eats its eggshell, and then begins feeding on the host plant. A caterpillar spends this stage of the butterfly life cycle consuming massive amounts of food, shedding its exoskeleton (skin) as many as five times as it becomes larger.

When the caterpillar reaches full size, it enters a protected stage of development inside a chrysalis. During this nonfeeding phase, it is known as a pupa. Inside the chrysalis, the metamorphosis from a caterpillar into a butterfly occurs. This may happen over the winter.

After a butterfly emerges from its chrysalis, it will seek nectar from a variety of flowering plants, salts from mud, and sugar from tree sap or rotting fruit. As an adult, the butterfly will mate and start the cycle again.

A monarch butterfly takes nectar from a swamp milkweed (Asclepias incarnata). In this stage of its life cycle, it will feed, mate, and reproduce to start yet another butterfly life cycle.

Host plants for caterpillars in the Butterfly Habitat Garden include (above left and right) river birch (Betula nigra 'Heritage') and staghorn sumac (Rhus typhina).

The ENTRANCE on the Mall end of the Butterfly Habitat Garden is marked by native Virginia sweetspire (*Itea virginica*) winding around massive boulders to suggest passage into a wild, natural place. Here and throughout the garden, educational signs introduce butterfly gardening, explore the interaction between insects and plants, provide the plants' common and botanical names, and explain how plants figure in the life cycle of butterflies.

The WETLAND showcases native plants such as river birch (*Betula nigra*) that offer wind protection, food, and nesting sites. The black willow (*Salix nigra*) and other trees are larval hosts for many butterflies, including the viceroy (*Limenitis archippus*), a mimic of the monarch. Around the small pond, moist, shallow depressions allow for male butterflies to "puddle," an activity that enables them to draw nutrients such as salts from the damp soil. Here huge rocks absorb the sun's warmth and provide flat places for butterflies, which are cold-blooded insects, to bask and warm themselves.

A waterlily (Nymphaea sp.) floats on the surface of a pond in the wetland area. Around the pond, butterflies "puddle" in moist depressions to draw nutrients from the soil.

The MEADOW brims with native grasses and wildflowers, including purple coneflowers (*Echinacea purpurea*) and butterfly weed (*Asclepias tuberosa*). A succession of native perennials bloom from spring to fall, affording a long season of nectar plants for adult butterflies. Red clover (*Trifolium pratense*), the host plant of the orange sulphur butterfly (*Colias eurytheme*), is one of the plants that offer shelter and food for larvae. A swath of native little bluestem (*Schizachyrium scoparium*) traversing the meadow provides dense sheaves of tall grass blades, places preferred by butterflies for laying eggs.

The WOODLAND EDGE simulates those places in the wild that occur between open meadow and dense forest canopy. Here in the light shade of native species—redbud (*Cercis canadensis*), prickly ash (*Zanthoxylum americanum*), and low shrubs such as highbush blueberry (*Vaccinium corymbosum*) and chokeberry (*Photinia pyrifolia*)—butterflies find places to hide and cool off in hot weather. They are often found perching on the trunks of trees and feeding on sap. At the base of shrubs and trees, false nettle (*Boehmeria cylindrica*) and other low herbaceous plants offer food for caterpillars, including larvae of the red admiral (*Vanessa atalanta*). Columbine (*Aquilegia canadensis*), a good nectar plant, thrives in this section in partial shade.

The BACK-YARD garden is designed to show visitors how to attract butterflies to their own home gardens. It features plants that are commonly available from local nurseries and garden centers. Excellent examples of plants that attract butterflies to the home are herbs such as chives (*Allium schoenoprasum*), mint (*Mentha* sp.), rosemary (*Rosmarinus officinalis*), and sweet fennel (*Foeniculum vulgare*), a favorite of swallowtail caterpillars.

In the Butterfly Habitat Garden's back-yard section, the flowers of tall verbena (Verbena bonariensis) and Joe Pye weed (Eupatorium purpureum) draw butterflies to their nectar (above left and right).

Staffs of the National Museum of Natural History and Smithsonian Gardens advise that butterflies are more likely to appear in a home garden if these steps are followed:

Garden organically. Remember that pesticides, even natural herbicides, are harmful to butterflies.

Go native. Learn which butterflies live in your area, and then plant the host plants that will attract them.

Diversify. Use a mixture of trees, shrubs, and herbaceous plants to provide shelter and food.

Swaths of native wildflowers—including black-eyed Susans (Rudbeckia sp.), coneflowers (Echinacea sp.), and wild bergamot or bee balm (Monarda fistulosa)—advertise their presence in the garden and draw butterflies.

Advertise. Add multiples of colorful nectar plants for the adult butterflies. The bigger the patch, the more likely that butterflies will see it and be drawn to your garden.

Puddle mud. Create a low, muddy depression that will give male butterflies a place to puddle.

AMERICAN ELMS

Popular, fast growing, and easy to obtain, American elm trees (*Ulmus americana*) were once the dominant feature of many towns. Residential streets would become spectacular green cathedrals when the wide-spreading branches of elms met overhead. Washington's nickname "City of Trees" probably derives from the prevalence of elms along its streets and in its public places. The McMillan Plan of 1901 specified that elm trees be planted in four rows fifty feet apart as street trees and as a unifying element on the Mall. Elms were later planted on the Ellipse, in Potomac Park, and around the Jefferson and Lincoln Memorials.

It is estimated that some 77 million elms grew in cities and towns across the United States before 1930. In that year, Dutch elm disease appeared in Cleveland, Ohio. Three years later it was discovered in New York; in 1947, on the grounds of the Lincoln Memorial; and in 1952, on the Mall. Thousands of diseased trees were replaced with Princeton elms, cultivars that are resistant to Dutch elm disease. The elms on the National Museum of Natural History's almost five acres are among the 192 specimens that can be seen today on the Smithsonian grounds.

Soaring, majestic American elms (Ulmus americana) turn bright yellow in the fall and then bear tiny red flowers the following spring. Close to two hundred of them still grace the Smithsonian Gardens, among them this elm on the National Museum of Natural History's grounds.

109

Heirloom and Victory Gardens

Fittingly for a museum that chronicles the American experience, the landscaping around the National Museum of American History includes two gardens that feature plants from American gardens of the past. The Heirloom Garden presents classic flowers and herbs that have been grown for generations. The Victory Garden commemorates the food gardens that supported the war effort during World War II.

The Heirloom Garden

Visitors coming to the museum from the Mall will cross the spacious south terrace en route to the museum entrance. All along the terrace, nearly a third of an acre of raised beds brim with the shrubs and flowers that compose the Heirloom Garden. A walk along the terrace can be a stroll down memory lane, made all the more nostalgic by American music from various eras that is piped into the garden.

Designed by the Smithsonian Gardens landscape architects Paul Lindell and Karen Swanson, the Heirloom Garden opened in 1998. The plants chosen for its raised beds are ones that grew in American gardens from colonial times until 1950, when the use of hybrids became widespread and agricultural practices became more industrialized. Plants in the Heirloom Garden are either natural species (ones that have not been "improved" by breeders) or varieties that have long been cultivated. What all the plants have in common is that they are open pollinated (not hybrids), meaning that they reproduce the characteristics of the parents when raised from seed.

Heirlooms are plants from the past with a past. They are the herbs, vegetables, and flowers that the colonists and other early settlers cultivated so carefully in the eighteenth century for "meate or medicine" and "for use or for delight." They are the herbs that George Washington grew at Mount Vernon and the flower seeds that Thomas Jefferson traded with friends. Heirloom plants were sprouted from treasured seeds and bulbs carried from European homelands to America, where they put down roots and prospered. Later they were dug up from homesteads and transplanted to the back yards of new houses in urban and suburban neighborhoods. Typically not used by modern, large-scale agriculture, heirloom plants have been passed along from great-grandmothers to grandfathers to mothers to children to neighbors. In each new place, they have managed—by virtue of strong constitutions—to survive, thrive, and delight. Each time they are grown, their genes are passed on and add to the biodiversity of the species.

Visitors to the Heirloom Garden approaching from the Mall are greeted with a terrace featuring Japanese wisteria (Wisteria floribunda). Long lived and long a treasure in American gardens, it is stunning when its pendant lavender flowers bloom in the spring.

The perennials, biennials, bulbs, and annuals that populate the Heirloom Garden are tried-and-true plants that have been grown and handed down for generations. They include (opposite) mallows (Malva 'Zebrina'), valerian (Centranthus ruber 'Jupiter's Beard'), and chives (Allium schoenoprasum) in a composition of pinks and reds.

America's gardening past comes alive in the Heirloom Garden. Spring is bright with bulbs such as daffodils. 'Sir Watkin,' a meteoric breakthrough in the 1880s that brought size and strong color into the breeder's palette, has large, cupped yellow flowers that stand up to twenty-four inches tall. 'Thalia,' another old hybrid that is sometimes called "the orchid narcissus," is derived from *Narcissus triandrus*. The pure snow white flower dates from 1916. In ancient times, white daffodils were associated with death and called grave flowers. This aura has clung to them, and some people still consider white daffodils unlucky to bring into the house; nonetheless, 'Thalia' has remained popular for its beauty and reliability. Another daffodil in the Heirloom Garden dates from around 1600: 'Pheasant's Eye' (*Narcissus poeticus recurvus* 'Pheasant's Eye'). Pictured in old English herbals, it got its name from the red and yellow rim around a green eye in the center of sparkling white petals. 'Pheasant's Eye' is fabulously fragrant.

Pretty, tough, and easy to grow from seed, nasturtiums (Tropaeolum majus 'Vesuvius') were brought to Europe in the late fifteenth century by Spanish conquistadores.

No sooner have the daffodils faded than the rest of the garden springs to life with annuals and perennials. Columbines (*Aquilegia* sp.), iris (*Iris* sp.), love-in-a-mist (*Nigella damascena*), scented pelargonium (*Pelargonium* sp.), and hollyhocks (*Alcea* sp.) are a few of the familiar old favorites that populate this garden. 'Painted Lady,' the first bicolor sweet pea (*Lathyrus odoratus*) available, was introduced in the United States no later than 1811. That year Thomas Jefferson, an avid plant enthusiast, planted it at Monticello, his Virginia estate. Nasturtiums (*Tropaeolum majus*), harvested by Spanish conquistadors in Peru, eventually made their way to England and returned to the New World with colonists.

In the spring, yellow columbines (Aquilegia chrysantha) are in full bloom in the Heirloom Garden (opposite top), while their garden mates—purple sage (Salvia officinalis 'Purpurea') and crape myrtles (Lagerstroemia × hybrida)—are in leaf.

Summer brings cheerful annuals (opposite bottom), such as zinnias (Zinnia acerosa 'Cut and Come Again') and coleus (Solenostemon Giant Exhibition 'Rustic Red').

English daisies (Bellis perennis), the original he-loves-me-he-loves-me-not daisy, have been beloved and a symbol of rebirth since the Middle Ages. Shasta daisies (Leucanthemum × superbum), a perennial species developed by Luther Burbank in the late nineteenth century, are much larger than English daisies. In the Heirloom Garden, Shasta daisies mingle with hardy annuals such as cornflower blue bachelor's buttons (Centaurea cyanus 'Jubilee Gem'), an All-America Selections winner from 1937; multicolored Victorian coleus (Solenostemon scutellarioides) varieties; and bells of Ireland (Moluccella laevis), an annual with tiny, fragrant, orchidlike flowers in the center of large green calyxes (the outer protective cover of flowers).

Planted in the garden beds are herbs that have been used throughout history as medicine. Some, such as lavender (Lavandula sp.) and thyme (Thymus sp.), were picked from ancient to medieval times to treat depression. Others, such as feverfew (Tanacetum parthenium), addressed headaches and fevers. Yarrow (Achillea millefolium) was called "herba militaris" in antiquity because it stanched the blood from wounds suffered in battle. Cowslips (Primula veris) were a headache and cough remedy and were also made into wine. Chamomile (Chamaemelum nobile), brewed into tea, is still used to calm stomachs and induce rest. Peonies (Paeonia lactiflora), which were grown in the Far East and considered panaceas for just about everything from toothaches to evil spirits, were also prescribed in the United States at the turn of the twentieth century for chorea, epilepsy, spasms, and various nervous afflictions.

Feverfew (Tanacetum parthenium) figured in seventeenth-century herbals as a remedy for headaches. Medical scientists are now learning that its compounds may indeed be effective for migraines.

Crape myrtles (opposite, Lagerstroemia 'Sioux' shown) provide a unifying element in the Heirloom Garden, softening the building's mass and shading the heirloom flower underplantings. Zinnia 'Crystal Palace' and Petunia 'Surfinia Sky Blue' bloom in the foreground.

Sage (shown is a purple form, Salvia officinalis 'Pupurea') got its name from the belief of ancient Greeks and Romans that it imparted wisdom and mental prowess. It was used in the Middle Ages as a treatment for memory loss, among other ailments.

The Victory Garden

The Stars and Stripes Cafe on the lower level of the National Museum of American History opens onto the spacious Victory Garden. This vegetable garden recalls the World War II era, when the government promoted gardening and canning as a patriotic duty to help save the nation's farm products for the armed forces and the American Allies. Slogans such as "Food will win the war and write the peace" and "The plow line is the battle line" spurred this effort. "A Victory garden is like a share in an airplane factory," stated Claude R. Wickard, secretary of agriculture under President Franklin D. Roosevelt. "It helps win the war and pays dividends too."

In addition to encouraging home gardens, the government set up a rationing system to ensure that the armed forces received the resources they needed to fight and that food and fuel were divided fairly on the home front. Sugar, butter, eggs, milk, cheese, red meat, coffee, and canned foods were all rationed. These restrictions also meant that Americans' traditional recipes had to be altered.

The victory garden movement caught fire. Although a similar program had been in place during World War I, it was during World War II that growing food became one of the greatest volunteer efforts the country had ever witnessed. Nearly twenty million garden plots—approximately one for every six people— were planted in back yards, school yards, parks, empty lots, and even window boxes. Seed purchases rose by 300 percent, and the sale of pressure cookers used for canning fruits and vegetables skyrocketed. Americans organized, pooled resources with neighbors, formed cooperatives, and were overwhelmingly successful in raising produce. The U.S. Department of Agriculture estimated that near the end of the war, 44 percent of America's vegetables were grown in victory gardens. Approximately eight million tons of produce were harvested, an amount equal to commercial production. The gardens were so successful that produce shortages occurred in the months after the war's end, because in the euphoria, people scaled back their growing of vegetables.

During the World War II era, eye-catching posters encouraged Americans to grow and preserve their own vegetables. Victory gardening was considered a patriotic activity, one widely promoted by the federal government.

The Victory Garden at the National Museum of American History, adjacent to the Stars and Stripes Cafe, features a wide variety of heirloom vegetables (opposite).

Lettuce

One of the most ancient of vegetable crops, lettuce is easy to grow and early to harvest. In 550 BCE, Herodotus wrote of Persian kings enjoying *Lactuca* at their royal tables. The Latin genus name *Lactuca* refers to lettuce's milky sap. Although the Greeks thought that lettuce caused male impotence, the Romans took a different view. They introduced lettuce, which they believed to be an aphrodisiac, as a first course. It was poached in or dressed with heated oil and vinegar.

A hardy annual, lettuce was cultivated in England beginning in the mid-sixteenth century and brought to America by the colonists. One of the varieties that grow in the Victory Garden, named 'Red Deer Tongue,' is among the oldest in the United States, having been introduced around 1740. Others include Bronze Arrow, considered by many to be the most delicious of all, and 'Tennis Ball,' a black-seeded lettuce planted by Thomas Jefferson at Monticello. Jefferson noted that it did "not require as much care and attention" as other types. The ancestor of Boston lettuce (a variety of Butterhead lettuce), 'Tennis Ball' was usually pickled in salt brine and served as a side dish.

Bronze Arrow lettuce (Lactuca sativa), a venerable variety growing in the Victory Garden, is considered to be among the most delicious.

D'Anjou pear trees (Pyrus communis 'D'Anjou') are espaliered along the wall of the Victory Garden, as are apple trees in other locations.

The Victory Garden at the National Museum of American History is inspired by a 1940s victory garden. At about 130 feet long by 20 feet wide, it supports more than fifty classic vegetable varieties as well as fruit trees. Espaliered against the back wall are one D'Anjou and one Bartlett pear tree (Pyrus sp.) as well as young 'Arkansas Black,' 'Lady,' and 'Wolf River' apple trees (Malus domestica), also trained as espaliers. At the base of the trees are rows of vegetables, most of them dating back much further than the 1940s, and all have stories to tell:

Mortgage Lifter tomatoes (Solanum lycopersicum) are an old variety yielding delicious fruits that can weigh more than two pounds each.

Dating from the 1930s, the Mortgage Lifter tomato (Solanum lycopersicum) came by its name honestly. It actually freed its creator, M. C. Byles of Logan, West Virginia, of his mortgage. Nicknamed "Radiator Charlie," Byles crossed different varieties of the biggest, meatiest tomatoes he could find over six seasons, producing a super tomato with delicious fruits averaging more than two pounds apiece. He sold plants at one dollar each, an exorbitant price at the time. Nevertheless, sales were brisk, and he paid off his $6,000 mortgage in six years.

Root vegetables that could be stored over winter were crucial to early Americans, who faced a period called "the six weeks of want" each year. From the end of January to the middle of March, if they exhausted their stores of vegetables, there would be little to eat until spring. Beets were among the most popular vegetables in the diet of seventeenth- and eighteenth-century Americans, and one of the vegetables the colonists were able to store well was the Early Blood Turnip beet, now one of the oldest surviving varieties from the eighteenth century. This beet derives its name from its often early maturity and the thick, red juice it exudes during cooking.

An eggplant (Solanum melongena) growing in the Victory Garden thrives in the sunshine of Washington's long, steamy summers.

Thomas Jefferson named the Arikara pole bean for the Dakotas' Arikara tribe, which shared them with Lewis and Clark during their Voyage of Discovery. The dried beans were a vital source of food for the exploratory party during the grueling winter of 1805 at Fort Mandan. At Monticello Jefferson later grew the beans, which could also be eaten as snap beans, and described them as "forward," because they bore early.

An African American heirloom from the Chesapeake Bay area, the fish pepper is esteemed by pepper aficionados. The attractive green and white variegated plants bear cream and green striped peppers that mature red and hot. They are used to make a paprika to flavor a delicious white sauce that is excellent with seafood.

Attractive and productive, pole beans (Phaseolus vulgaris 'Dow Purple Podded') climb up handmade string trellises in the Victory Garden (opposite).

Introduced in 1926 by Peter Henderson and Company, the Moon and Stars watermelon has a deep green shell patterned with large and small yellow spots: the moon and stars. It fell out of favor, and by 1980 people feared that the seeds no longer existed. And then in 1981, Merle Van Doren of Macon, Missouri, contacted Kent Whealy, cofounder of the Seed Savers Exchange, a nonprofit organization dedicated to preserving heirloom varieties, and gave him some seeds. The Southern Exposure Seed Exchange reintroduced the melon as the Amish Moon and Stars in 1987. Unlike modern melons, bred for a convenient absence of seeds, the delectable Moon and Stars watermelon makes up in taste for the presence of seeds.

All the vegetables, fruit, and herbs in the Victory Garden are grown organically. The horticulturist Joe Brunetti plants a cover crop, such as winter rye, in the fall. In early spring the cover crop is tilled into the ground to enrich the soil. Crops are rotated; nitrogen-fixing beans follow heavy feeder crops, such as tomatoes and corn. Companion planting helps keep insects at bay. Fertilizing with compost provides the soil with millions of microorganisms and beneficial fungi to achieve healthy plants and habitat. Some of the organically grown vegetables and herbs harvested from the Victory Garden make their way into the kitchen of the Stars and Stripes Cafe. Tomatoes, sweet and hot peppers, beans, eggplant, and herbs are a few of the foods the chef has turned into dishes served in the restaurant overlooking the garden.

Although the Victory Garden commemorates the home front effort during World War II, it continues to be relevant today given the resurgence of vegetable gardening. Maintained organically, it uses winter cover crops and compost for fertilizer.

While the National Museum of American History's Victory Garden tells the story of one important aspect of the home front during the 1940s, it remains relevant today. A desire for high-quality, healthful organic produce that is locally grown to conserve resources has spurred a nationwide interest in organic gardening. The Victory Garden presents a successful example of what home gardeners themselves can accomplish.

Outside the National Museum of American History, red oak (Quercus rubra) *street trees have been transplanted from places that figured prominently in American history. This example comes from Manassas National Battlefield Park in Virginia.*

RED OAKS

Along the museum's Constitution Avenue entrance, young red oaks (Quercus rubra) serve as street trees. Complementing exhibits inside, the red oaks have been transplanted from places that figured in American history, such as Nantucket Island, once home to a vibrant whaling industry; Lexington Green in Massachusetts, site of the first armed conflict between Minutemen and the British on April 19, 1775; and the Connecticut family estate of the patriot Nathan Hale (1755–76), who was hanged by the British as a spy. Some came from along the Trail of Tears, representing the journey Native Americans took westward after being forced from their homes by the Indian Removal Act of 1830. Others were taken from the Illinois family estate of Robert Kennicott, who collected and catalogued for the Smithsonian and lived in the Smithsonian Castle with other naturalists during the Civil War. Trees also represent Manassas Battlefield (also called Bull Run), where the first major land battle of the Civil War was fought on July 21, 1861.

ROBERT AND ARLENE KOGOD COURTYARD

DONALD W. REYNOLDS CENTER FOR AMERICAN ART AND PORTRAITURE

On one of Washington's cold, gray, rainy days, a nice place to stop for a cup of coffee or to enjoy lunch is the glass-covered courtyard shared by the National Portrait Gallery and the Smithsonian American Art Museum. This courtyard of one of Washington's oldest architectural landmarks was originally open to the air, with a pair of spreading elms and two fountains. When the new courtyard welcomed its first visitors on November 18, 2007, it instantly took its place among the city's largest event venues and earned the distinction of being named "one of the new seven architectural wonders of the world" by *Condé Nast Traveler*.

Covering the courtyard shared by the Smithsonian American Art Museum and the National Portrait Gallery allowed the creation of a new interior environment. Beneath its undulating glass and steel canopy, delicate scrims of water, white marble planters, and well-spaced trees now invite visitors to linger regardless of the season.

The National Historic Landmark that houses the two museums, which was the home of the U.S. Patent Office from 1840 to 1932, was begun in 1836 in the Greek Revival style by the architect Robert Mills (1781–1855), who also designed the Washington Monument. It was not completed until 1868, thirty-two years later, by Thomas Ustick Walter (1804–87), the designer of the U.S. Capitol dome. Covering an entire city block between F and G and Seventh and Ninth Streets, Northwest, its size manifested the importance of the Patent Office during an era when technological invention drove the national economy and began to mold the American character. Walt Whitman, who read to wounded soldiers when it was used as a military hospital during the Civil War, called it "the noblest of Washington's buildings." It was the site of President Abraham Lincoln's second Inaugural Ball in 1865.

Before the canopy was installed, tulips (Tulipa 'Apricot Beauty') bloomed in the open-air court-yard. Amid the sculpture in the background was an American elm (Ulmus americana).

By 1953, despite being one of Washington's most historic buildings, the aging structure was scheduled for demolition. Concerned preservationists protested, and their voices were heard. President Dwight D. Eisenhower signed legislation in 1955 that saved the building from becoming a parking lot. Three years later Congress formally transferred the landmark to the Smithsonian. After renovations, the building opened in 1968 as the home of the Smithsonian American Art Museum in the north wing and the National Portrait Gallery in the south wing. A recent renovation (2000–2006) showcased the landmark's architectural features, including porticoes modeled after the Parthenon in Athens, a curving double staircase, vaulted galleries, large windows, and skylights as long as a city block.

When the enclosed courtyard was unveiled in 2007, it was under a massive new roof and had a new name, the Robert and Arlene Kogod Courtyard, honoring donors who are Washington art collectors and philanthropists. The glass and steel canopy—a distinctive modern accent to the venerable Greek Revival structure—was designed by the renowned British architect Norman Foster of Foster + Partners, noted in part for adding contemporary additions to historically important buildings. Among his many works in fifty countries are the glazed cupola on the new Reichstag (German Parliament) in Berlin and the glass-roofed Great Court of the British Museum in London.

The architect and his associates worked with the Smithsonian to create an innovative enclosure for the 28,000-square-foot space that was sensitive to the landmark, all the while adding a modern element in keeping with the building's role as a "temple of invention." Foster described the process as "driven by deep respect." As a result, the earthquake-proof, undulating canopy, composed of 864 double-glazed pieces of glass he designed, does not touch the building at any point. Instead the glass "float[s] above it like a cloud," supported by eight aluminum-clad columns. Foster's respect for the past was rewarded. At the World Architecture Festival held in Barcelona in 2008, Foster + Partners won top honors in the "New and Old" category for inserting a modern element into a historic building.

Under Foster's canopy was a new landscape, designed in association with him by the internationally noted landscape architect Kathryn Gustafson of Gustafson Guthrie Nichol in Seattle, Washington. In place of the original fountains, Gustafson installed a series of four of her signature water scrims. Thin, imperceptibly tilted planes of black granite were sunk one-quarter inch into the courtyard floor. A diffuse sheet of water flows over each scrim—just enough to give a sheen of water to the paving, mirror the canopy above, and dampen the soles of a visitor's shoes. When large events are scheduled, the fountain feeding the scrims is shut off, the water drains away, and the floor remains dry.

Subtle yet compelling scrims of water, designed by the landscape architect Kathryn Gustafson, flow over tilted planes of black granite. The trees in the marble planters are black olives (Bucida buceras).

Gustafson also designed long, white, gracefully curved marble-faced planters that are in keeping with the building's Greek Revival architecture and enhance the courtyard's serene atmosphere. The plants in the planters, which also serve as seating, have a traditional, temperate look yet are able to survive life under a glass roof in a year-round temperature of about 72 degrees Fahrenheit. In the abundant natural light, subtropicals, including seventeen 'Shady Lady' black olive trees (*Bucida buceras* 'Shady Lady') and a thirty-two-foot-tall Florida rusty fig tree (*Ficus rubiginosa* 'Florida'), native to Australia, share the planters with ground covers of ferns, shrubs, and flowering plants.

The Kogod Courtyard's dining area (opposite) is surrounded by trees, shrubs, and flowers growing in marble planters. Shadow play from the ribbed canopy constantly transforms the interior space.

The large rusty fig tree (Ficus rubiginosa 'Florida'), in the center, is a native of eastern Australia, where it is a popular street tree. It typically grows to about thirty feet tall and produces fruit that ripens red.

Outside the Donald W. Reynolds Center for American Art and Portraiture, along the Seventh Street facade, this hackberry—a moderately fast-growing hardwood tree—has distinctive warty, corklike bark and produces long-lasting red to purple berries in the fall. Hackberries (Celtis occidentalis) grow to about fifty feet tall with rounded crowns and can live 150 to 200 years.

On occasion the palette is expanded with unusual shrubs, such as coffee plants (*Coffea arabica*) and bold tropicals. During the winter holiday season, brilliant red poinsettias (*Euphorbia pulcherrima*) contrast with white Amazon lilies (*Eucharis grandiflora*) that waft their sweet fragrance into the courtyard. The show-stopping Amazon lily hails from South America. Its shiny, deep green foliage is attractive even when the flowers are not blooming. Related to the *Amaryllis*, Amazon lilies are grown from bulbs that thrive in the courtyard's moderate temperature.

A display of clivia (*Clivia miniata*) follows, bringing cheerful color and the promise of spring to winter's darkest days. At other times, flamingo flowers (*Anthurium scherzenianum*), ixora (*Ixora coccihea*), and stromanthe tricolor (*Stromanthe sanguinea* 'Triostar') add vivid and welcome color.

The rich hues, textures, and fragrances of the plants contribute immeasurably to the courtyard's atmosphere. A tranquil oasis in the midst of Washington's busy Penn Quarter neighborhood, the Kogod Courtyard is magical by night. When the sky darkens, the planters are illuminated and lights in the canopy overhead sparkle like stars.

BLACK OLIVE TREES

Popular street trees in South Florida, the 'Shady Lady' black olives in the Kogod Courtyard were shipped in climate-controlled, covered flatbed trailers from Florida, a two-day trip. Each of the seventeen trees weighed approximately two thousand pounds and was lowered into the courtyard by a tower crane through a twelve-foot opening in the canopy. This opening was designed to accommodate material too large to carry through the museums.

Black olive trees (*Bucida buceras*) are an evergreen species native to Mexico's Yucatán and to Central and South America. Despite the common name, black olives are not members of the olive family and do not produce olives; instead the name derives from small, hard seed capsules produced on the trees after flowering. Black olives belong to the *Combretaceae* family of tropical flowering plants. Prized for their spreading umbrella shape, leathery whorled leaves, handsome trunks, and drought tolerance, they grow up to twenty feet tall and bear fragrant yellow flowers in the spring. The cultivar 'Shady Lady' has smaller, tidier leaves on gracefully layered branches, has a more constrained growth habit, and does not produce seeds.

Along the far wall are black olive trees (Bucida buceras), beautiful and fragrant when their yellow flowers bloom and handsome year-round with small evergreen leaves and a wide, spreading crown. Shefflera 'Amate' grows in the foreground.

OTHER GARDENS
OF THE SMITHSONIAN

In addition to the ten Smithsonian gardens on or near the Mall, two other notable garden spaces figure prominently in the Smithsonian's diverse repertoire of museums. As the institution's reach began to extend beyond the Mall in the late nineteenth century, so too did its gardens. Visitors to the nation's capital and to New York City will find the following two museum sites worthy additions to their tour of the Smithsonian gardens.

GARDENS AT THE NATIONAL ZOO

Although the gardens at the Smithsonian's National Zoological Park are often upstaged by its four-legged inhabitants, they remain among the zoo's most enduring exhibits. The zoo, located on 163 acres of urban parkland nestled within Rock Creek Park in Northwest Washington, is home to four hundred animal species and thousands of plants, native and non-native. This fusion of plant and animal life sets apart the gardens at the National Zoo.

"Uncle Beazley," the friendly fiberglass triceratops, peeks out from a bed of tropical giant taro (Alocasia macrorrhizos) and papyrus (Cyperus papyrus) across from the National Zoo's Lemur Island.

The park's winding main path, Olmsted Walk, is named in honor of Frederick Law Olmsted (1822–1903), the renowned landscape architect who designed the zoo. When the National Zoological Park opened in 1890, Olmsted's innovative landscape plan marked an important departure from the nineteenth-century practice of confining zoological collections to limited areas. The National Zoo preceded the founding of the New York Zoological Park and Munich's Hellabrun Zoo, thus likely making it the first major zoo to be located in a spacious landscaped setting. The park's primary aim was not to entertain people but instead to preserve endangered animals indigenous to the United States. The zoo was created at a time when Americans were concerned about the supposed closing of the western frontier and the dominance of a new urban, industrialized society. Its animals were reminders to visitors of the disappearing American wilderness.

Surrounding the animals is an enduring exhibit—the thousands of trees that line paths and provide habitats for native animal species. Some have stood since before the zoo existed, while others are saplings, planted weeks ago. Beautiful and wild—from Japanese zelkovas (Zelkova serrata) to white oaks (Quercus alba)—more than two hundred genera help create an urban refuge in the capital.

Among the zoo's gardens are some that emphasize the relationship between plants and animals. The Pollinarium, a greenhouse attached to the Invertebrate Exhibit, contains twoflower passionflower (Passiflora biflora), blue porterweed (Stachytarpheta jamaicensis), and other flowering plants pollinated by hummingbirds and bees that also inhabit the space. Just beyond the Pollinarium lies the

Butterfly Garden, full of butterfly weed (*Asclepias tuberosa*) and swamp milkweed (*Asclepias incarnata*) that attract monarchs (*Danaus plexippus*) as well as American painted ladies (*Vanessa virginiensis*), clouded sulphurs (*Colias philodice*), and snowberry clearwing moths (*Hemaris diffinis*).

Other gardens feature plant species that correspond to nearby animal exhibits or attractions. Surrounding "Uncle Beazley," the fiberglass triceratops sculpture across from Lemur Island, are giant taro (*Alocasia macrorrhizos*) and papyrus (*Cyperus papyrus*), descendants of plants that existed in the age of dinosaurs. At Kids' Farm, a pizza garden displays plants that are used for favorite foods. Horticulturists cultivate wheat, tomatoes, peppers, herbs, and olive plants to show visitors that a garden can be more than just a collection of blossoms—proving that it can also provide sustenance.

The zoo's gardens—telling stories about topics from urban woodlands to African grasslands, from life in the Amazon to East Asian forests—present thousands of plants and animals in a natural environment, cared for by the zoo's own horticulture staff. The experience communicates the importance of nature to the welfare of both people and animals, providing special insight into the relationship between the animal and plant kingdoms.

Inside the zoo's Pollinarium, a greenhouse adjacent to the Invertebrate Exhibit, is an indoor garden that highlights the relationships between plants and animals.

Arthur Ross Terrace and Garden, Cooper-Hewitt, National Design Museum

The Smithsonian's Cooper-Hewitt, National Design Museum is housed in the Andrew and Louise Carnegie Mansion, a national and New York City landmark located on Fifth Avenue at Ninety-first Street in Manhattan. The sixty-four-room house, designed by the architecture firm Babb, Cook and Willard in the comfortable style of a Georgian country house, was built between 1899 and 1902. When the Carnegies purchased land for their house in 1898, they purposely bought property far north of where their peers were living. Open space enabled them to build one of New York City's largest private gardens, designed by the celebrated landscape architect and engineer Richard Schermerhorn Jr. The house's main rooms were placed to face the rear garden, which remains a beautiful urban oasis across from Central Park, in what is now the middle of Manhattan's Museum Mile.

Andrew and Louise Carnegie's sixty-four-room mansion featured one of New York City's largest gardens. Now home to the Cooper-Hewitt, National Design Museum, the Fifth Avenue landmark is the namesake of the Carnegie Hill Historic District.

Today named the Arthur Ross Terrace and Garden, the garden is surrounded by a tall iron fence with impressive granite posts. A central lawn is bordered by a formal walk, and to the east a path cuts through a more heavily planted rockery (rock garden). Although the locations of the paths and beds are original, documentation of the initial planting scheme is missing. However, Louise Carnegie was known to have grown a variety of flowers and plants, including rhododendron (including azaleas), Chinese wisteria (*Wisteria sinensis*), flowering crabapple (*Malus* sp.), and ivy (*Hedera* sp.). Tended for the past eighteen years by the landscape designer Mary Riley Smith, the garden brims with shrubs, grasses, and perennials whose diverse foliage and flowers maintain seasonal interest.

Bright annuals bloom in spring and summer. In early May, long lavender panicles entwine four iconic wisteria vines, first planted for the Carnegies, that climb the mansion's southern facade; seasonal plantings of pink, lavender, and white tulips (*Tulipa* sp.) complement the wisteria blooms. In June the flower borders are lush with perennials such as clematis (*Clematis texensis* 'Duchess of Albany'), peonies (*Paeonia* sp.), iris (*Iris ensata* and *I. germanica*), balloon flower (*Platycodon grandiflora*), phlox (*Phlox paniculata*), and daylilies (*Hemerocallis* hybrids); in addition, many varieties of hosta, liriope, fern (*Athyrium nipponicum* var. *pictum* and *A. filix-femina*), and coral bells (*Heuchera micrantha* var. *diversifolia* 'Palace Purple' and *H.* 'Venus') weave a textured tapestry under the trees. Shrubs that create a backdrop for smaller perennials and annuals include Japanese barberry (*Berberis thunbergii* 'Crimson Pygmy'), variegated English holly (*Ilex aquifolium* 'Aurea Marginata'), and evergreen cherry laurel (*Prunus laurocerasus*), which provide color all season. Pink-flowered Japanese spirea (*Spirea japonica* × *bumalda* 'Anthony Waterer'), three types of hydrangea with large blue or white flower panicles, and rose of Sharon (*Hibiscus syriacus*) bloom in July and August. Ornamental grasses create bold punctuations throughout the borders.

After the flush of flowers is finished, annuals planted in late May carry the garden through to frost. The color scheme changes from year to year, typically including several varieties of salvia in pink and lavender tones, large- and small-flowered petunias, and tobacco plants (*Nicotiana* sp.) that fill the beds with color until winter comes, the gardens are cut back, and tulip bulbs are planted for the next year's spring display.

No longer are passersby limited to merely looking in through hedges along the fence to appreciate the Carnegies' garden. In the spaces once lovingly overseen by Louise, neighborhood residents today regularly visit the Arthur Ross Terrace and Garden to relax or soak up the sun. Where festive spring and summer tea parties were held a century ago for the Carnegies' friends, New Yorkers now can enter to read their newspaper at leisure.

In the spring, the conservatory on the mansion's southern facade (below left) looks out at a towering wisteria vine and beds of cheerful tulips and pansies.

The terrace of the museum is festooned with wisteria (below right). Beds of tulips are punctuated with deep ruby barberry shrubs (Berberis thunbergii 'Crimson Pygmy').

Plant Production and Exhibitions

The Smithsonian greenhouses (opposite) shelter thousands of tropical plants that are circulated into museum exhibits and outdoor horticultural displays. Working mostly behind the scenes, the plant production staff plants, installs, and routinely refreshes all the container plants and hanging baskets in the Smithsonian gardens (below).

Visitors to the Smithsonian museums are treated to outstanding gardens, landscaping, and interior displays. Few people probably have any idea of the behind-the-scenes efforts that keep these horticultural exhibits healthy, interesting, and beautiful. They may wonder, Where do all these plants come from and how do they get here? Where does a thousand-pound tropical tree spend the winter? Where do the orchids reside when they are not at peak bloom? The answers to these questions rest with a branch of Smithsonian Gardens called Greenhouse Nursery Operations. With responsibilities as varied as the propagation of plants including tropicals and orchids, interior plant display and care, and special events, sixteen staff members and some thirty volunteers do it all.

PLANT PRODUCTION

The seasonal plant production unit—charged with growing thousands of bedding and display plants and making hundreds of hanging baskets—works closely with Smithsonian Gardens horticulturists who submit designs for the museum gardens. Once a design is approved, the production staff plans the best way of producing the desired plants economically and within available space in the greenhouses. More than seventy thousand bedding plants are produced each year for the museums' flower beds and gardens. (Most are grown in pots on trays that are 100 percent biodegradable or in plastic containers that are recycled.)

The hundreds of hanging baskets in the Enid A. Haupt Garden and along Jefferson Drive, changed seasonally three times each year, are started in the production greenhouses. Hundreds of poinsettias for interior holiday displays are begun there in May and June. Because the plants come into bloom when daytime and nighttime lengths are approximately equal, it is crucial to maintain the hours of complete darkness—which in the past involved turning off the streetlights outside the greenhouses and requiring staff to turn off car headlights when approaching or leaving the greenhouses at night during poinsettia season. Unusual plants that are difficult to find in the trade—such as the heirloom plants for the Heirloom and Victory Gardens, small numbers of exotic plants, trial plants, and very expensive plants—are given priority in the production greenhouses.

This ixora (Ixora coccihea) is one of the plants grown by the production staff especially for the butterflies in the Butterfly Pavilion at the National Museum of Natural History.

The production unit also supplies tropical flowering plants for the butterflies in the National Museum of Natural History's Butterfly Pavilion. Entitled "Butterflies + Plants: Partners in Evolution," this exhibition, opened in 2008, enables visitors to walk through an indoor tropical garden among some three hundred butterflies from all over the world. Rotated into the exhibition on a weekly basis to ensure the freshness of the food-producing flowers, the varieties chosen are specific to the butterfly species on display. Ixoras and pentas are among the five hundred nectar- and pollen-producing plants grown in the Smithsonian greenhouses. For the safety of the butterflies, no pesticides with residual effects are used. After their time in the Butterfly Pavilion, the plants are destroyed to eliminate the potential introduction of insects and diseases.

Plants are also grown by the unit for the National Museum of Natural History's Insect Zoo. These plants can serve as either food or habitat for the zoo's inhabitants. Tomato plants, for example, become delectable fare for the zoo's tomato hornworm caterpillars.

During the growing season, hanging baskets and other containers in the gardens (opposite) brim with colorful petunias (Petunia). In the winter, lampposts and baskets are decorated with evergreens.

INTERIOR PLANT DISPLAYS

Horticultural displays featuring flowering plants in rotation, permanent tropical installations, and temporary special exhibits inside more than a dozen Smithsonian museums are the province of the interiors unit of Greenhouse Nursery Operations. One of the most widely noticed events for which the staff designs and installs displays is the winter holiday season, extending from Thanksgiving until the second week in January. Selections such as evergreen trees and seasonally appropriate flowers, among them blue coleus, poinsettias, and white moth orchids, typically form stunning displays.

Museum curators rely regularly on this unit to design with plants that enhance the impact of a particular exhibit as well as expand on its theme. When the National Museum of the American Indian holds its Chocolate Festival, for example, the interiors staff provides not only the chocolate trees (Theobroma cacao) but also plants that grow in tropical climates with chocolate, such as guava (Psidium sp.) and avocado (Persea americana). For the Hawaiian Festival, exhibits are augmented with plants important in Hawaiian culture, including taro (Colocasia esculenta), ginger (Zingiber officinale), and varieties of hibiscus. For an exhibit on the history of Panama in the S. Dillon Ripley Center, native Panamanian bromeliads and orchids were highlighted. Another exhibit there featured Chinese bonsai, called penjing, in miniature landscapes.

Interiors staff set up numerous horticultural displays in the museums, such as this pink quill (Tillandsia cyanea), and maintain them on a rotating schedule.

Greenhouse horticulturists must be familiar with the cultural requirements of an immense variety of tropical plants. Among the hundreds of tropicals in the greenhouses are rare exotics that have come from subtropical climates such as those of Florida, California, and Hawaii. These plants are grown to exhibit size under glass in the winter and moved outside into the gardens for display in the summer.

Many of the museums are decorated for the winter holidays with festive poinsettias and evergreens (opposite). This display is in the National Museum of Natural History's monumental rotunda.

Many of the plants grow to be huge trees. Moving hundreds of large specimens into museum displays is no easy task—each one typically requires the use of a forklift. In the early morning before a museum is open to the public, plants destined for a display are moved out of the greenhouse, placed in a truck, and taken to the museum, where they are unloaded and installed before the first visitor arrives. This is only the beginning, as the interiors unit then sets up a rotating schedule to groom and tend the horticultural displays. Every day staff members travel to some of the museums to conduct their housekeeping: pruning, dusting, and removing dead or damaged leaves and litter that has been tossed into the plants' pots. Sometimes displays are rearranged, and individual plants that are no longer attractive are replaced.

THE ORCHID COLLECTION

Smithsonian Gardens also maintains displays of orchids in cases in the National Museum of Natural History, the Castle, and the Ripley Center. Extremely diverse in its scope, the Smithsonian Orchid Collection, begun by Mary Livingston Ripley, includes more than eight thousand specimens carefully selected for their educational as well as ornamental qualities—from the tiny *Platystele*, with flowers the size of pinheads, to giants such as the sugar cane orchid (*Grammatophyllum speciosum*), which can grow twenty-five feet across. Specializing in New World genera such as *Cattleya*, *Laelia*, *Brassavola*, and *Sobralia*, the collection also includes African, Asian, and Australian taxa (a group with shared characteristics). Found on every continent but Antarctica, orchids are increasingly imperiled by habitat destruction.

The Smithsonian's renowned Orchid Collection numbers more than eight thousand plants. Housed in climate-controlled greenhouses, the orchids are rotated into museum displays or featured in the decor for special events when they are at their peak bloom.

Many hardy native orchids, including lady's slippers (*Cypripedium* sp.), grass pinks (*Calopogon tuberosus*), rose pogonias (*Pogonia ophioglossoides*), and nodding ladies' tresses (*Spiranthes cernua*), are being acquired by the Smithsonian as garden plants and may eventually figure in outdoor exhibits. Some of the finest specimens in the collection belong to the genus *Paphiopedilum*, a popular type of slipper orchid. These impressive specimens mingle with other fine orchids from around the world in an amazing array of sizes, flower shapes, and colors and show a fascinating range of survival strategies.

Ticoglossum krameri is a rarely cultivated Costa Rican endemic species that bears shell pink flowers, an unusual color for oncidioid orchids. The genus name refers to the colloquial term that Costa Ricans bestow on themselves, "Ticos."

Because a majority of orchids bloom in late winter and early spring, Smithsonian Gardens, the United States Botanic Garden, and often other departments of the Smithsonian collaborate on an orchid exhibition, held alternately at the Smithsonian or the Botanic Garden conservatory every year from January to April. The theme of each exhibition is educational, revealing specific aspects of orchid biology, history, and culture as well as the Smithsonian collection's vast scope. One year an exhibition entitled "Orchids: Take a Walk on the Wild Side" featured orchids one might encounter on a hike in the tree canopy, accurately illustrating their natural habitat and raising awareness of the need for their conservation. Another year, "Orchid Express" used model trains to depict an orchid's journey from mountain tops to florist shops—a "kid-friendly" exhibition that reached out to visitors of all ages. "Nature's Jewels: A Living Exhibit of Orchids and Butterflies" vividly illustrated the relationship among orchids, butterflies, and other orchid pollinators. It was an interdisciplinary feat that could have been accomplished only by creative and cooperative staffs, and it served as a trial run for the National Museum of Natural History's exhibition "Butterflies + Plants: Partners in Evolution." Occurring during the bleakest months of the year, these popular exhibitions are wonderful opportunities to see stunning examples of some of the twenty-five thousand species of orchid that live in the wild.

Orchids from the collection, which are rotated into displays every three weeks when they are at peak bloom, may also find their way into floral decorations designed by the special events unit. Smithsonian museums and divisions as well as outside companies and organizations host hundreds of functions and receptions each year that are held after hours in the museums amid fabled exhibits. The special events staff enhances the venues with everything from tabletop centerpieces to large palms and ficus trees, all of which coordinate with event themes and are supplied by the greenhouses.

Orchid Survival Strategies

Orchids have evolved an amazing variety of adaptations to ensure their survival. To attract fly pollinators, for example, *Bulbophyllum echinolabium* sends out the potent stench of rotten flesh. Even more unnerving are the flowers of this orchid, which can grow to fifteen inches in length. The petals and sepals (petal-like parts of the calyx) are long and graceful, but the center of the flower, technically a *labellum* (third petal), looks as if the orchid has ingested all but the masticated rear end of a dead mouse. Native to Borneo and Sulawesi, this orchid has a bloom period of about six months.

Myrmecophila, a name derived from the Greek words *Myrmec* (ants) and *phila* (to like), is a species with large pseudobulbs, storage organs that develop along the rhizomes of sympodial orchids (those that spread laterally). In *Myrmecophila* the hollow pseudobulbs provide a home for ants. They also presumably protect the orchids from other insects and thirsty larger critters in their seasonally desertlike habitat.

To ensure pollination, some *Oncidioid* orchids such as *Miltonia* (syn. *Oncidium*) *phymatochilum* produce myriad flowers that dance in the breeze. Aggressive bees mistake them for insect intruders and attack. As they do so, the bees come into contact with pollinia, globs of pollen that adhere to the bees.

Most people are familiar with vanilla flavoring if not its natural source (*Vanilla planifolia*), an evergreen vine native to Mexico and Central America. This orchid belongs to a circumtropical genus that includes about a hundred species. The Aztecs flavored their chocolate with vanilla, and the Spanish subsequently brought it to Europe. Now used around the world in cooking, vanilla is derived from what are called vanilla beans. Actually not beans at all, they are long seed capsules that develop after the plant flowers.

Bulbophyllum echinolabium attracts flies (its pollinators) by producing the odor of rotting carcasses.

Myrmecophila christinae (opposite top) is a stunning large orchid with fragrant flowers. Meaning "ant lover" in Greek, Myrmecophila refers to stinging ants that inhabit the plant's hollow pseudobulbs and keep thirsty predators away from the succulent plant in its seasonally dry habitat.

Hailing from the orchid-rich Macas region of Ecuador, the subtly beautiful Cyrtochilum macasense (opposite bottom) is probably one of the rarest orchids in cultivation in the world.

THE GREENHOUSES

Until the summer of 2010, the tasks of producing, designing, and maintaining beautiful plant displays inside and out, as well as decorating for special events, were accomplished in twelve antiquated greenhouses. Constructed between 1958 and 2000 and leased from the Armed Forces Retirement Home off North Capitol Street, the greenhouses were mostly manually operated. All unloading had to be done by hand because the structures had no loading dock. The kitchen of a small former caretaker's apartment served as library, lunchroom, and office space.

The Greenhouse Nursery Operations branch of Smithsonian Gardens has now moved into a state-of-the-art facility on a secure ten-acre lot within the Smithsonian's Museum Support Center in Suitland, Maryland. Included are fourteen greenhouses plus additional covered space that connects with administrative offices, a shade house, an outdoor growing area, and space for recycling. The greenhouses' environmental controls are programmed to maintain an ideal climate. A reverse-osmosis system removes solutes from water as it mists the greenhouses. Sensors close overhead vents, and a programmable shade cloth provides shade in summer and retains heat at night. A heated equipment room allows vehicles to be parked inside in cold weather to keep them warm enough to load plants. In short, the new facility has everything the old one lacked.

COLLECTIONS AND EDUCATION

A quiet alcove in the Enid A. Haupt Garden (opposite) is furnished with an antique bench and chair and ringed by tropical plants—a tall Abyssinian Red Ensete banana tree (Ensete ventricosum) and, at the lower right, a cut-leaf philodendron (Philodendron bipinnatifidum).

The Horticulture Collections Management and Education branch of Smithsonian Gardens serves as both a memory keeper and a tutor of gardening in America. Through its educational initiatives and programs, Smithsonian Gardens seeks to encourage the understanding and appreciation of gardens and horticulture, especially the ways in which they have intersected with and influenced American art, design, history, science, and culture. Collections ranging from photographic images and design records to furnishings and horticultural artifacts are regularly used by researchers and the general public to help explain or better understand the myriad stories that gardens have to tell. By preserving and interpreting the nation's garden heritage, Smithsonian Gardens underscores the importance of gardens in the American experience, especially how people use, transform, and enjoy their surroundings.

EDUCATION PROGRAMS

Smithsonian Gardens offers a wide variety of education programs for people of all ages. Here a staff horticulturist explains a beneficial insect release to two young visitors.

Education staff members develop interpretive programs and lectures, plan exhibits, and manage an online presence. Each year an active internship program hosts on average a dozen interns who work side by side with staff to gain practical professional experience. The Enid A. Haupt Fellowship in Horticulture supports full-time independent research; the work of Haupt Fellows has been published widely and used to create traveling Smithsonian exhibitions that highlight the American garden.

The Archives of American Gardens

Gardens are the most ephemeral of arts. Never static, they change from hour to hour, week to week, year to year—subject to change, loss, and destruction. The Archives of American Gardens, established in 1987, is a collection that captures the essence of thousands of American gardens in eighty thousand images, historical records, and plans. Some of these records fix a moment in the life of an existing garden, while others describe gardens that have been lost forever.

The Archives grew from the early efforts of the first director of Smithsonian Gardens, James R. Buckler, to collect historical records relating to garden nurseries and seed companies. Its mission has since evolved: the unit now collects, preserves, and makes available for research use documentation relating to a wide variety of cultivated gardens throughout the United States. Holdings include images and documentation for both historic and contemporary gardens, ranging from the simplest of cottage plots to grand estates.

At the core of the Archives is a collection that was a gift from the Garden Club of America in 1992. It consists of three thousand hand-colored glass lantern slides dating from the 1920s and 1930s and thousands of 35 mm slides from after the 1960s. Today the Garden Club of America Collection includes more than forty-five thousand images of historic and contemporary gardens. Designers of these gardens range from preeminent landscape architects to novice enthusiasts. Collection images regularly appear in magazine and newspaper articles, exhibitions, Web pages, educational materials, and books.

The Garden Club of America has been an active supporter of the Archives since its founding. Each year, scores of field volunteers from this organization document gardens to add to the GCA Collection. About fifty gardens throughout the United States—small and large, decorative and utilitarian, classical and vernacular, simple and ornate—are added annually to the archival holdings. The sheer range of designs helps chart how garden tastes, trends, resources, and uses have evolved over time.

This image from the early 1920s of a young woman with 'Emily Gray' roses is from the rosarian and photographer J. Horace McFarland's collection, now included in the Archives of American Gardens. McFarland's Harrisburg, Pennsylvania, garden was used as the backdrop for this and hundreds of other images that illustrated nursery and seed catalogs published by his printing firm.

THORNEWOOD

Thornewood, home of the banker Chester A. Thorne (1863–1927) on the shores of American Lake in Tacoma, Washington, is captured in its heyday in the Garden Club of America Collection's hand-colored glass lantern slides. The sunken English-style garden that Chester and Anna Thorne commissioned for their English Tudor mansion in 1908 was carved out of the Northwest wilderness by the Olmsted Brothers. This landscape architecture firm incorporated sweeping views of Mount Tacoma (now known as Mount Rainier) by placing the walled garden on an axis with the peak. The long walks, borders, and boundary walls all led one's eyes to a splendid mountain vista. The use of specific color plantings, orchestrated by Albert Hart of Kew Gardens in England, created dramatic seasonal effects. Unsurprisingly Thornewood was voted the most beautiful garden in the United States by the Garden Club of America in 1930.

As with many of the grand estates, Thornewood eventually became too costly to maintain. In 1959 the 100-acre property was subdivided into thirty lots. By the 1980s the view of Mount Rainier from the original garden was obstructed by trees. The bones of the sunken garden, including a brick wall and steps, still held clues to the property's former opulence, but the plantings were overgrown and neglected. Fortunately the walled garden was eventually revived. Today the property is run as a historic country inn.

Documentation such as this in the Archives of American Gardens serves as a reminder of the importance and evolution of our nation's garden heritage.

Colors were painted by hand onto this glass lantern slide of Thornewood, lending it a slightly ethereal quality. It is just one of many important pieces of evidence documenting the garden's history.

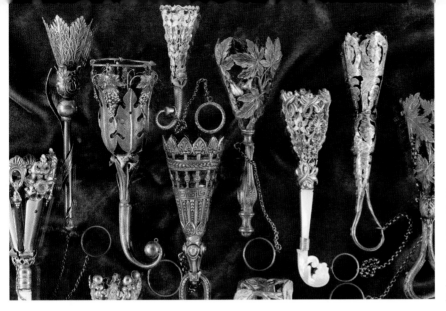

THE GARDEN FURNISHINGS AND HORTICULTURAL ARTIFACTS COLLECTIONS

The Smithsonian's Garden Furnishings Collection came into being in 1973, just a year after the Office of Horticulture was established. The Victorian Garden adjacent to the Castle called for outdoor furniture that complemented its elaborate design, making cast-iron furnishings from the Victorian era a natural choice. Since then more than 1,700 antique furnishings and horticultural artifacts have been acquired by Smithsonian Gardens. Dozens of these furnishings are in use in the Enid A. Haupt, Mary Livingston Ripley, and Kathrine Dulin Folger Gardens. Decorative urns hold arrangements of plants and flowers, while antique cast-iron benches and settees provide resting spots for visitors and nearby office workers on their lunch breaks. Two nineteenth-century fountains, also of cast iron, cool the air, muffle street noise, and attract birds to the Ripley and Folger Gardens.

Items in the complementary Horticultural Artifacts Collection include bouquet holders, wire floral frames, advertising materials, seed boxes, florist accessories, and gardening tools. Of particular note is the Frances Jones Poetker Collection, which includes more than 250 delicate bouquet holders. During the Victorian era, these popular fashion accessories displayed flowers that communicated in a language all their own. Floral dictionaries served as sourcebooks for an elaborate lexicon of courtship, in which emotional sentiments or moods were conveyed through the wearing or offering of particular flowers. Bluebells, for example, signified kindness, while rosemary symbolized remembrance.

Although the language of flowers belongs to the past, as do items in the Garden Furnishings and Horticultural Artifacts Collections and in the Archives of American Gardens, they also inform our future by preserving for posterity a distinctly American gardening heritage.

Antique urns from the Smithsonian collections are displayed throughout the gardens. This one in the Ripley Garden (opposite) is planted with asparagus fern (Asparagus densiflorus 'Meyersii').

Selected Bibliography

Blue Spruce, Duane, and Tanya Thrasher, editors. *The Land Has Memory*. National Museum of the American Indian. Chapel Hill: University of North Carolina Press, 2008.

Burleigh, Nina. *The Stranger and the Statesman. James Smithson, John Quincy Adams, and the Making of America's Greatest Museum: The Smithsonian*. New York: William Morrow, 2003.

Choukas-Bradley, Melanie, and Polly Alexander. *City of Trees: The Complete Field Guide to the Trees of Washington, D.C.* 1987. Revised edition, Charlottesville: University of Virginia Press, 2008.

Dickens, Charles. *American Notes: A Journey*. 1842.

Reprint, New York: Fromm International, 1985.

Ewing, Heather. *The Lost World of James Smithson: Science, Revolution, and the Birth of the Smithsonian*. New York: Bloomsbury, 2007.

Ewing, Heather, and Amy Ballard. *A Guide to Smithsonian Architecture*. Washington, D.C.: Smithsonian Books, 2009.

Field, Cynthia R., Richard E. Stamm, and Heather P. Ewing. *The Castle: An Illustrated History of the Smithsonian Building*. Washington, D.C.: Smithsonian Institution Press, 1993.

Fletcher, Valerie J. *A Garden for Art: Outdoor Sculpture at the Hirshhorn Museum*. Hirshhorn

Museum and Sculpture Garden. London: Thames and Hudson, 1998.

Hyams, Barry. *Hirshhorn: Medici from Brooklyn*. New York: E. P. Dutton, 1979.

Lawton, Thomas, and Linda Merrill. *Freer: A Legacy of Art*. Freer Gallery of Art. New York: Harry N. Abrams, 1993.

Park, Edwards, and Jean Paul Carlhian. *A New View from the Castle*. Washington, D.C.: Smithsonian Institution Press, 1987.

Savage, Kirk. *Monument Wars: Washington, D.C., the National Mall, and the Transformation of the Memorial Landscape*. Berkeley: University of California Press, 2009.

In the greenhouses, boots at the ready await a busy day of work by Smithsonian Gardens staff. On call 24 hours a day, personnel respond to garden emergencies ranging from snowstorms and downed tree limbs to broken irrigation lines.

ACKNOWLEDGMENTS

Smithsonian Gardens is grateful to the many individuals who have assisted with the preparation of this book. First and foremost is the author, Carole Ottesen. Working with enthusiasm and passion for the gardens of the Smithsonian, she expertly researched the facts and gently coaxed out the impressions of each garden to write this exceptional guide.

We are especially grateful to the Smithsonian's Office of Facilities Management and Reliability and the Smithsonian Institution Scholarly Press for providing funding necessary to publish the book. We also thank the Friends of the Smithsonian for their enthusiastic support.

A special thank you is due Nancy Bechtol, director of the Office of Facilities Management and Reliability, for her support and encouragement; Joyce Connolly, Kelly Crawford, and Paula Healy of Smithsonian Gardens, for their careful proofreading and coordination of images and photography; Diana Bramble, Joe Brunetti, Bill Donnelly, Graham Davis, Janet Draper, Shelley Gaskins, Jonathan Kavalier, Joel Lemp, Paul Lindell, Brett McNish,

Tom Mirenda, Christine Price-Abelow, Melanie Pyle, Michael Riordan, Jeff Schneider, and Rick Shilling of Smithsonian Gardens, for sharing their intimate knowledge of the plants, collections, and programs within each garden and for reviewing each garden chapter.

During the research and review of this book, many colleagues were called on for assistance. Thank you to Amy Ballard and Pam Henson, who reviewed the draft manuscript from a historical perspective. Representatives from each museum made crucial contributions in the review of their museum's respective chapter, among them Pamela Baker-Masson, Laura Baptiste, Bethany Bentley, Tom Crouch, Nathan Erwin, Terry Erwin, Valerie Fletcher, Lee Glazer, Gary Hevel, David Hogge, Paula Johnson, Caroline Jones, Chuck Kim, Jodi Legge, Sally Love, Tanya Thrasher, Peter Winkler, and Bill Yeingst.

Very special thanks go to the Smithsonian Institution photographers whose handsome work is included here, especially, Eric Long and Ken Rahaim, who devoted so much to this

project. Our appreciation goes to the National Air and Space Museum for sharing Eric and his time with us. We were indeed fortunate to work with him, as his patient manner and skills produced beautiful images that highlight the splendor of the Smithsonian gardens.

The seed of an idea for this book was first planted with the late Caroline Newman of Smithsonian Books. In her characteristically enthusiastic manner, Caroline responded with gusto to the idea. We hope that she would have been pleased with how well this book turned out. Since Caroline's passing, Carolyn Gleason of Smithsonian Books has guided the project's development to publication. Sincere thanks are due Carolyn, an avid gardener and editor extraordinaire, and to Christina Wiginton of Smithsonian Books, who kept us on track.

We are also most grateful to have worked with the book's designer, Robert L. Wiser, and the editor, Diane Maddex of Archetype Press.

As with any organization, its people are its lifeblood, and this is particularly true of

Smithsonian Gardens. In the division's relatively short history, many gardeners, horticulturists, volunteers, and interns have contributed to the evolution of the institution's gardens. Listing all of those who through the years have helped make the gardens what they are today would be impossible, and we ask forgiveness for any omissions. But we would like to recognize those who currently toil daily to enrich the Smithsonian and its visitors through their work in the exceptional gardens, horticultural exhibits, collections, and education programs. They are Michael Allen, Joe Brice, Cindy Brown, Tom Brown, Erin Clark, James Clark, Francis Cooper, Victoria DiBella, Allison Dineen, Kurt Donaldson, Randy Dudley, Matthew Fleming, Vanessa Garner, Jill Gonzalez, Tom Hattaway, Sarah Hedean, Kevin Hill, Shannon Hill, Stanley Hilton, Monty Holmes, Meredith Hubel, Sean Jones, Cheyenne Kim, Ed Kunickis, Sherri Manning, George Morgan, Darlene Price, Daniel Russell, Jeff Smith, Alexandra Thompson, and Sarah Tietbohl.

Barbara Faust, Associate Director
Smithsonian Gardens

INDEX

The figures in Always Becoming (2007), an organic sculpture near the south entrance of the National Museum of the American Indian, are highlighted by the late-afternoon sun.

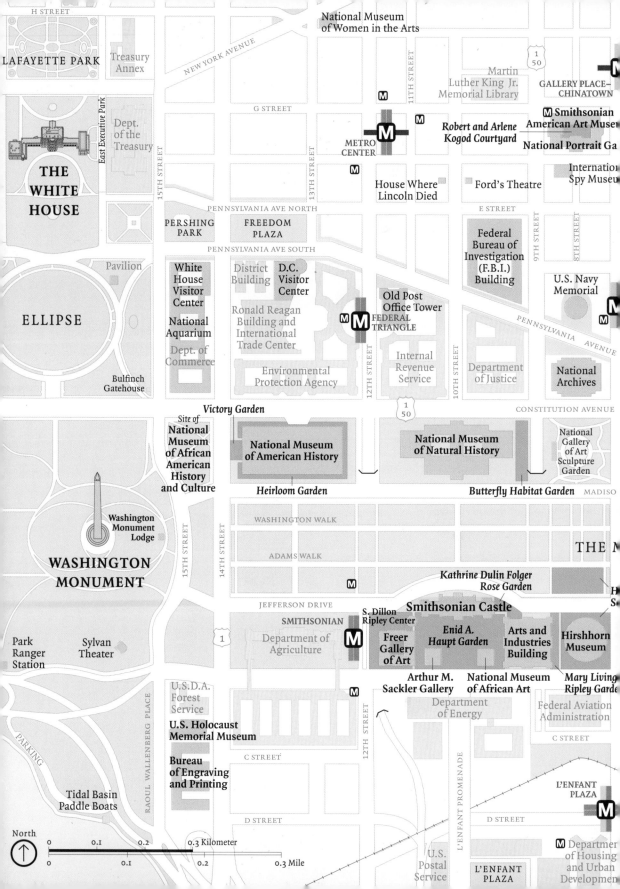

H STREET

LAFAYETTE PARK

Treasury Annex

NEW YORK AVENUE

National Museum of Women in the Arts

Martin Luther King Jr. Memorial Library

GALLERY PLACE–CHINATOWN

G STREET

11TH STREET

METRO CENTER

Robert and Arlene Kogod Courtyard

Smithsonian American Art Muse

National Portrait Ga

East Executive Park

Dept. of the Treasury

THE WHITE HOUSE

15TH STREET

House Where Lincoln Died

Ford's Theatre

Internation Spy Museu

13TH STREET

E STREET

PENNSYLVANIA AVE NORTH

PERSHING PARK

FREEDOM PLAZA

Federal Bureau of Investigation (F.B.I.) Building

9TH STREET

8TH STREET

PENNSYLVANIA AVE SOUTH

ELLIPSE

Pavilion

White House Visitor Center

National Aquarium

Dept. of Commerce

Bulfinch Gatehouse

District Building

D.C. Visitor Center

Ronald Reagan Building and International Trade Center

Environmental Protection Agency

Old Post Office Tower

FEDERAL TRIANGLE

12TH STREET

1 50

Internal Revenue Service

10TH STREET

U.S. Navy Memorial

PENNSYLVANIA AVENUE

Department of Justice

National Archives

CONSTITUTION AVENUE

Victory Garden

Site of National Museum of African American History and Culture

National Museum of American History

Heirloom Garden

National Museum of Natural History

Butterfly Habitat Garden

National Gallery of Art Sculpture Garden

MADISO

Washington Monument Lodge

WASHINGTON MONUMENT

15TH STREET

14TH STREET

WASHINGTON WALK

ADAMS WALK

THE M

Kathrine Dulin Folger Rose Garden

H S

JEFFERSON DRIVE

Park Ranger Station

Sylvan Theater

1

SMITHSONIAN

Department of Agriculture

S. Dillon Ripley Center

Smithsonian Castle

Freer Gallery of Art

Enid A. Haupt Garden

Arts and Industries Building

Hirshhorn Museum

Arthur M. Sackler Gallery

National Museum of African Art

Mary Living Ripley Garde

RAOUL WALLENBERG PLACE

U.S.D.A. Forest Service

U.S. Holocaust Memorial Museum

Bureau of Engraving and Printing

12TH STREET

Department of Energy

L'ENFANT PROMENADE

Federal Aviation Administration

C STREET

PARKING

C STREET

L'ENFANT PLAZA

Tidal Basin Paddle Boats

D STREET

D STREET

M

L'ENFANT PLAZA

North

0   0.1   0.2   0.3 Kilometer
0   0.1   0.2   0.3 Mile

U.S. Postal Service

Departmen of Housing and Urban Developmen

L'ENFANT PLAZA